I0132524

Abby Has Issues

Humor essays and unsolicited opinions from
www.AbbyHasIssues.com

Abby Heugel

Abby Has Issues

FIRST EDITION

ISBN: 0983719195
ISBN-13: 978-0-9837191-9-9

DEDICATION

To my mom, who has always been my biggest fan and biggest genetic contributor to my neurosis.

On both accounts, I'm forever in your debt.

Abby Has Issues

CONTENTS

Page

1   My Marriage Proposal
4   Shiny Things Distract Me
8   Roughing It
11 Smiling Is My Favorite
15 So Many Issues, So Little Time
17 Why I Don't Have a Reality Show
20 Uncle June
22 Bug Off
24 Wax On, Wax Off
27 My Internal GPA is MIA
29 Forecast: Sunny With a Chance of Jazz Hands
32 A Suggestion to My Coworkers Who Procreate
34 Backseat Driver
37 Everything Must Go
40 Vegucation
42 Being Punctual
45 Don't Sweat It
48 You're a Weirdo, But That's Okay
51 At the Car Wash
54 CSI: Pond/Fountain Thing
58 Velcro Rollers, Eyelash Ass
61 Snowpocalypse
63 That's Where You Came From
67 Purses and Pillows and Pumpkins, Oh My!
70 When the Question is the Answer
72 Beware the Mall
75 Power to the People
78 Ironing Out the Details
82 Swiffer Sink Saga of 2011
85 Farmers Mark-etiquette
88 False Advertising

Part 2: From What I Can Recall

90 Dear Tooth Fairy
92 Bus 315
95 Simple Math
98 Birthday Hit List
101 It Was a Drive-By Beaching
104 Vive la France
107 The Graduate
109 Summer Rhyme Time
112 Exercise TV and Me
115 Dog Day Detour
118 My Fuzzy Little Soul Sister
122 Yes, I'm Nosy
124 A Good Nine Lives
127 Help Me Plan My Midlife Crisis
130 More…Infinity
133 Senior Moments
138 Senior Moments: Bingo
141 Our Scars
143 Senior Moments: Opening Day
146 My Perfect Game
148 Senior Moments: Dating
151 A Toast

FORWARD

This is the page where I tell you wonderful things about myself so you continue to read these essays.

The short version is that I'm a magazine writer and editor with "issues" not only of the magazine variety, but also in the form of OCD, a rabid interest in sports, farmers markets in the summer, yoga, things that make me laugh, the occasional strong drink and my own bed.

And asparagus. And avocado. And lots of other green things.

The longer version is that I have needed a creative outlet my whole life, and it just so happens that people will occasionally pay me to write words. After graduating with a degree in professional writing, I went on to experience everything from freelance sports writing and non-profit communications to being an editorial assistant for a professional sports team.

The past five years I have been a writer and editor of national trade publications. I contribute more than 100 nationally published features a year and am responsible for all additional editorial content of the magazines, websites and enewsletters.

While my days are spent writing serious content in an effort to pay my mortgage and keep my produce supply fully stocked, my favorite projects allow for creativity and humor, which is why I started a blog two years ago.

With my own little piece of the World Wide Web, I share my neurotic take on everything from the small woodland creatures that both terrorize and amuse me to old people throwing tater tots at my head.

I can get serious and introspective, but I try and keep it light.

Because my knowledge of technology is limited to hitting "publish" and calling tech support, I decided I wanted a collection of my words I could hold in my hand, something I couldn't accidentally delete while looking for a vegan cheesecake recipe on the Internet.

Plus, my grandma stories are too good to keep to myself.

The result is the collection you are currently reading, and I apologize for the pictures. They look better on the blog.

But I also thank you for helping me reach my goal of eventual world dominance. You see, my ultimate goal is to become independently wealthy so I can live on an island where I work on my exotic container gardens while tirelessly devoting myself to perfecting the slow motion "Baywatch" jog.

Or eat an entire meal without spilling on myself.

I have issues.

Sincerely,

Abby Heugel

MY MARRIAGE PROPOSAL

I'm generally low maintenance, but the same cannot be said for my house.

As any homeowner can attest, the things that need to be done around a house are not only numerous, but often never-ending. And unless you enjoy changing air filters, scrubbing out the shower or replacing the rain gutters, these tasks are not something one often looks forward to doing.

Side note: While I do love cleaning and have an unnatural affinity for my Swiffer Wet Jet and 'Ove'Glove—best thing ever—this love does not extend to various other jobs that require my attention, or more accurately, require me to ignore because I have no clue how to do them.

Because I'm single, I either have to figure out how to put the screen doors in and replace *(insert random odd thing you didn't even know existed until it broke)* myself, or bribe someone to do it with beer or brownies.

I'm lucky that my family lives close by because they help with odds and ends, but I have to admit there are times when I think it would be nice to have a man around to fix a thing or two, change the oil in my Blazer and possibly help with the bills. Don't get me wrong in that I work hard, have no problem working hard and am proud of everything I have, but not thinking about these annoying tasks would be great.

So I think I have found the perfect solution—I have decided I want to be a Trophy Wife. Well, I should rephrase that to be a bit more accurate:

I have decided I want to be a Consolation Prize Wife.

A Consolation Prize Wife is like a Trophy Wife, but actually way cooler because she requires less maintenance.

The typical Trophy Wife is young and married to an older powerful man—the Sugar Daddy— and serves as a visual status symbol of his success. She's basically arm candy.

I'm not quite as young or as hot and probably come with more issues, but despite being skinny with no boobs, I can clean up nice. So even though I missed my chance to land a Sugar Daddy with one foot in the grave and another on a banana peel, I'm thinking I might be able to swing the alternative here.

The Consolation Prize Wife

As a Consolation Prize Wife, I would still marry a powerful man and serve as a visual *(or vocal, more likely)* status symbol of his humble success *(like I said, I make a great party date.)* He wouldn't be old, but would still have money so that I could be a stay-at-home-mom minus the kids, do yoga to stay in physical and emotional shape, write an engaging and witty blog and oversee the management of our animal rescue center.

I would be required to get dressed up and attend various social events with him, tell him he's cool and frequent the Farmers Market on a weekly basis for the things I would learn how to cook. In return, he would be required to be handy around the house, request no emotional attachment or sexual interest unless provoked *(by me)* and have a Canadian accent.

And we would have separate beds, as I love to sleep much more than I love to spoon.

This way my grass would get cut, I could write and be my own boss, consider it a professional obligation to clean everything all the time and keep myself in shape. He would get to always have a witty plus-one for events, someone to keep things running smooth at home while he does the work thing and the freedom to never have to answer the questions "Why do you love me" or "What are you thinking about right now?"

Why?

Because I'm smart and fairly secure, so there's no question about why he would love me. And second, I don't really care what he's thinking about right now unless it involves a) cleaning the gutters, b) urging me in his Canadian accent to go write or c) my next feeding.

After all, just because a house is high maintenance doesn't mean I have to be. And as a Consolation Prize Wife, I will make it my duty to remain that way until death do us part, at which time I will be back to where I started from.

Which will be, most likely, Home Depot.

SHINY THINGS DISTRACT ME

Alternate title: *Sharing my OCD—Obscure Creative Directives*

Get inspired to write something brilliant at a completely inopportune time. Forget about it for a bit.

Start doing something else, remember your idea and head into the living room to turn on your computer.

While waiting for it to boot up, go into the kitchen to make a cup of tea.

The water takes a minute to heat up. Notice that the shelf next to the sink is dusty, grab a rag and quickly wipe it down.

This leads to cleaning the whole counter, as the power of Lysol 4-in-1 knows no bounds.

Remember the water is boiled and make your cup of tea.

Head back into the living room *(still inspired.)*

Focus.

Decide to check your email for just a second before really settling in for the composition of brilliance.

Twenty minutes and a witty Facebook status update later, return to your writing.

Write without self-editing. Just write.

Realize you have the word "spatulate" stuck in your head and decide that yes, it can be used in a sentence.

The word "spatulate" makes you think of cake, which reminds you of the Sara Lee commercial, the jingle of which is now stuck in your head.

Remember that until you saw it in print, you thought it was "Nobody does it like Sara Lee" because "Nobody doesn't like Sara Lee" is a double negative and doesn't make as much sense.

Focus; not on the grammatical shortcomings of the Sara Lee Corporation.

Start writing and soon realize you forgot about your tea, so go into the kitchen and throw it in the microwave.

Fill the 30 seconds by getting your lunch containers ready for the next day, and while you're at it, fill the lunch containers so you're good-to-go.

Notice the shelf in the fridge could stand to be wiped down. Call in Lysol 4-in-1 again; its power knows no bounds.

Remember about the tea, retrieve said tea and head back to the computer.

Focus. Write a bit.

Bite your tongue—literally.

Tea makes you pee, so go relieve the problem—among other things.

Wash your hands and decide to replace the Glade Plug-In in the outlet.

While in the closet, take note of the Swiffer and decide it's time to go for a ride.

Turn the radio on—loud—not because it's a mandatory step, but because it makes you happy.

Swiffering also makes you happy, so clean, sing and dance around your kitchen with your freak flag flying high.

The floor needs to dry, so head back into the living room.

Remember you were writing.

Turn the radio down. Find yourself humming.

Bite your tongue again in the exact same spot. Curse—loudly—not because it's a mandatory step, but because it makes you feel better.

Turn the radio off.

Focus.

Write without self-editing. Just write.

Decide you don't want to overdo it, so hit "save" and go put the kitchen rugs back on the *(clean)* floor.

While you're throwing things, throw your yoga mat on the living room carpet as a reminder that you are going to do it later. If the mat is on the floor, you will do it later.

Light the "Fresh Baked Cookies"-scented candle in your living room, not to set a romantic mood for yourself, but to make it smell like delicious baked cookies you didn't bake *(as nobody does it like Sara Lee has given you a temporary inferiority complex.)*

Return to your computer and read what you wrote without judgment, and then read what you wrote with the addition of judgment.

Decide it's not brilliant, but it's you.

Marvel at how much that candle really smells like Fresh Baked Cookies and resist the urge to lick it.

Focus.

Attempt to add an image into your blog post, as you've heard that people like to see images in posts.

Shrug and decide you don't care what people like to see in posts. You can't please them all.

Reread your words one more time.

Brush off self-doubt and embrace what you are.

Hit "publish."

Start doing something else until you get inspired to write something brilliant at a completely inopportune time—maybe yoga.

Repeat.

ROUGHING IT

Many people pack up and go camping. I am not one of them, as I do not camp

Don't get me wrong. I love the outdoors and worship the sun and nature. And while I'm not high-maintenance—*the closest thing I've had to a pedicure in the past few years is stubbing my toe while falling UP the stairs and losing a nail*—I don't find appeal in sleeping on the ground in a tent pretending I'm homeless.

While it's been years since I've been on vacation, when I go, it involves the option of a warm shower, a real bed and little bottles of shampoo I can steal and take home with me.

And although I've never slept in a tent, I do have a bit of camping experience. When I was younger we had a trailer up north that we spent a good deal of time at in the summer. It was a decent sized rig with a shower, small kitchen, deck, etc., but it was still a trailer.

I fished, I shot my bow and arrow *(not at anything living, at least on purpose,)* I tore around on the 4-wheeler, we went for nature walks and into town for ice cream at Jones' ice cream and cheap toys at the Ben Franklin.

We would blow up the inflatable alligator and hit the lake before coming back to nighttime campfires, Cribbage games and attempts to attract bats by throwing random crap up in the air by the park lights.

I was young, and other than the fact that I rolled out of the top bunk of triple bunk beds—a bed rail was quickly installed—I had no real complaints. Now that I'm older and debatably wiser, I would have many complaints, which is why I don't even attempt to pretend to want to camp.

Thesis statement:

Why someone would want to leave indoor plumbing, decent food and the likelihood of not contracting mosquito malaria for outhouses, dirt-covered food and the likelihood of being attacked by a baby deer in the woods is beyond me.*

*To each their own, of this I know *(disclaimer so campers don't get pissed, although if they're camping, they shouldn't have access to Wi-Fi.)*

But for those who enjoy camping and would like to recreate this experience at home, I have a few suggestions:

- Hang your clothes over a wood fire to get that signature smell, the one that will hopefully cover up the other signature smell of musty dampness.

- While you're over the fire, singe your eyelashes and grab a hot poker to recreate the experience of starting the fire and attempting to roast anything over said fire with a metal stick.

- Scald the skin on the roof of your mouth in an attempt to eat whatever it is you were trying to roast that didn't fall into the flame.

- Hover—a lot—and get used to swatting bugs with one hand while wiping with the other. This takes skill, which is why you will most likely find yourself pissing on your own leg *(hey, you wanted to go camping.)*

- Pour sand directly into the bottom of your bathing suit and any exposed crack or opening in your body. If a lake is nearby, also include seaweed.

- If you feel like getting fancy, spray yourself with a water bottle to recreate the *(lack of)* water pressure trailer showers provide. Forget about washing your hair *(this is actually a positive in my book.)*

- Plant families of the loudest bugs on the planet in your backyard directly next to your window. If available, add in the mating calls of mystery creatures you're sure are rabid and hunting you down.

- Roll your meals in damp dirt.

- Roll your clothes in damp dirt.

- Roll yourself in damp dirt.

So for those of you starting your camping season, may the force be with you. I plan on working in the yard a bit, reading and enjoying the luxury of warm showers, good food I didn't have to catch and a few good baseball games.

I love not camping.

SMILING IS MY FAVORITE

True story.

I had to buy a new phone and qualified for an upgrade discount, so I went to the Verizon store and bought a new one. When I got home, I had an email with an online offer that confused me. Thinking I got screwed out of money, I decided to participate in a "live support chat" session online.

I copied the text and pasted it below.

Please wait for a Chat Representative to respond.

Thank you for contacting Verizon Wireless. My name is 'Gina', how may I assist you?

Abby: I just returned home from the Verizon store because I was told I qualified for an upgrade. So I purchased the new phone, got home and just saw that there was an online discount for the same phone that I just bought! How can I get that $50 discount? It seems unfair to have to pay the full price if I'm a returning customer.

Gina: I'm sorry for the misunderstanding about online pricing vs. store pricing. I can gladly assist you.

(Insert boring details here.)

Gina: Thank you. First I wanted to mention so you understand why this happened. Stores have their own pricing. Now if you did purchase the phone at a company owned store I can see if I can credit your account.

Gina: One moment.

Gina: Great, you did upgrade at a company owned store. I'm trying to see what you paid for the phone. $30?

Abby: $(insert amount much greater than $30)!

Gina: Oh. Gosh. Thank you. Please give me a few moments.

(Insert a few moments here.)

Abby: I'm still here...

Gina: Good news. We are unable to match online pricing as it's for online orders only. Once you return you're phone, place the order in My Verizon and it will be free.

Abby: But I already cut the UPC off the box and sent it in for the rebate. And it's "your," not "you're," just for future reference. I'm not trying to be rude, but it's a pet peeve of mine.

Gina: Ha. Okay. You can still return phones after submitting the rebate. Your refund will be less the rebate.

Abby: So if I take the phone back, do they simply refund me what I paid for this phone and then I order the new one online for $X?

Gina: Yes, I see what you mean now. Hmm. The store will refund your money less the $50 rebate then you will get the $50 on a Visa card. Once they process your return, you can then order the phone in My Verizon for $X.

Abby: What do I tell them when I go there?

Gina: Exactly what you told me. Wait. You mentioned a $50 rebate. Online orders offer instant rebates and the stores instead have mail in rebates. In the end your price is still the same. I thought at first you found it was free.

Side note: Who mentioned a free phone?

Gina: Do you follow me?

Abby: Like on Twitter? I just starting Tweeting last week and don't really know what I'm doing.

Gina: Ha. No, not on Twitter.

Abby: In fact, it's kind of like this—typing back and forth—except you have to add in things like @ and # every once in awhile.

Gina: That sounds nice. Do you understand about the phone?

Abby: I think so. So there's no difference between ordering it online or in the store. One is with a mail-in rebate and one is instant, so this whole conversation was for nothing?

Gina: You were under impression that you would get an additional $50 off but online there's no mail-in rebate in addition. It would be worth it if you saw it was free online.

(pause)

Gina: I just caught that now. You never mentioned seeing a free phone online.

Abby: Right…so it's the same price either way then.

Gina: I guess so! Are you familiar with how to track your rebate submission online? I can give you the direct link.

Abby: I sent it in already. It will come in the mail. As long as I'm not getting screwed by ordering in store instead of online, I guess this whole thing was a moot point!

Gina: I'm glad it works out the same. I included the link above to help you track the status.

Abby: I just mailed it an hour ago, so I don't think I can check yet. However, I will keep the link for future use. Thanks.

Gina: Yes, exactly. Save it to your favorites.

Abby: Smiling is my favorite.

Gina: In 4-6 weeks you will receive your Visa card that can be used anywhere to further smiles!

Abby: Yay for smiles!

Gina: I hope you are enjoying your new phone. Did you have any additional questions or concerns for me at this time?

Abby: Thank you Gina. I plan on enjoying my new phone by not answering it when it rings and dying a little inside when the little text thing goes off.

Gina: You can change your text notifications in the Sounds setting menu if it is bothering you at the wrong times.

Abby: No, the people bother me. The noises are fine.

Gina: Oh no! Well you go and have a great peaceful day by yourself with lots of smiles. If you have no other questions, I thank you for being a valued Verizon Wireless customer.

SO MANY ISSUES, SO LITTLE TIME

Although I love a good book, I also love magazines.

Considering my attention span, that comes as no surprise. They are a very non-committal endeavor in that I don't have to dedicate large chunks of time to enjoy them. A column here, a two-page spread there, visuals to draw me in and feed me bits and pieces of information with bright pretty colors and fun fonts. Aside from being peppered with rogue subscription cards as I flip through, what's not to love?

Being the eternal realistic optimist, I have found something not to love — when all of the issues arrive on the same exact day.

While that might not have an effect on a less neurotic individual, we *are* dealing with me here. I subscribe to the four or five magazines. What that means is that a few days into a new month, I am suddenly overwhelmed with quality reading material.

It's like I go from famine to feast and I suddenly feel the need to go on a bender and read everything, just because it's there.

Each month I contemplate the option of rationing the issues out, but then I run the risk of rendering a timely story irrelevant. *(More with the sports magazines on this one, although it would be upsetting to be the last to know about a Real Simple new use for an old thing if the old thing could be used in a new way relevant to my current situation.)*

So I set them all on the table in my kitchen in no particular order and tell myself I will flip through them when I can, when the spirit moves me. This is much easier to accomplish when it's warm out, as I can take a cup of tea and sit on my deck.

But in the winter, it's more difficult. I will sometimes go to the gym and sit on a bike *(going nowhere despite my enthusiastic pedaling)* for 30 minutes, driven much more by the desire to burn through the pages of the latest issue than to feel the burn.

I'll get through one or two of the magazines within a week, but then I'll start to feel like I should "save" the rest for a bit. What I'm saving it for I have no idea. I just don't want to read the last one and then be without a magazine option.

What inevitably happens it that two weeks will go by and I'll realize that I still haven't read the latest issue of the one I was "saving." It's not that I didn't have the time, but rather that I didn't have the attention span—or the magazine got buried underneath a pile of other things thrown on the "throw all your crap here" table.

Sigh...

I told you I have issues.

WHY I DON'T HAVE A REALITY SHOW

Whenever the weekend approaches, people start talking with each other about their weekend plans—going out, heading up to the lake for one last weekend, getting together with friends and gossiping about the friends that aren't out with them, too.

Truth be told, I hate being asked what I'm doing because it's usually comparably lame. While I enjoy being social in small doses, I get more excited about plans being cancelled than I would if I actually participated in the plans. My perfect weekend is usually spent outside, putzing around the house, watching the games and generally not having to be anywhere at any time.

In other words, I will never have a reality show.

And thank goodness for Twitter, because I can prove my point with actual tweets from this past weekend. Now keep in mind that these aren't all my tweets. I did do actual stuff that went undocumented and I only tweet from my computer and not a phone super glued to my hand, but they give you a general chronological idea of how my Friday through Sunday was spent—in 140 characters or less.

The Tweet-end

Yes, thank you everyone for reminding me it's Friday and you're happy. In other news, restaurants serve food.

It's probably not a good thing to have left the house wondering if you remembered to put makeup on.

It's Friday. I'm going on a bender of the cleaning variety. This is why I don't have a reality show.

Forgetting to ventilate makes bonding with Scrubbing Bubbles much more interesting.

Stretching and carbo loading for the game tonight. You know, the one I'm going to sit on my ass and watch for three hours. #MLB

I would be a social butterfly if it didn't involve other people. And bras.

Her cat is on a leash, yet the children run free. Something's wrong with this picture.

If you steal my tomatoes, I will steal your tomatoes. You've been warned, crazy chain-smoking neighbor lady. You've been warned.

Maybe it's because I'm Polish, but I think babushkas need to make a comeback.

Even though I love them, steamed Brussels sprouts totally smell like urine.

It's raining and I feel lazy. I can't be certain, but I think there might be a correlation.

It stopped raining, so I have no excuse to be lazy. However, now back-to-back ballgames are on. I'm officially dating my couch.

Why are your teeth on the table? Don't throw ham! Hold it until we get back to your room! Did you just pinch me? Old people are exhausting.

Watched a squirrel for 10 minutes. Thought "Wow, squirrels are so easily entertained." Realized I just watched a squirrel for 10 minutes.

Growing up on Disney movies has left me so disillusioned about small woodland creatures and their willingness to help me with my chores.

I don't know what makes me sadder to see on my walk—road kill or a dropped and melted ice cream cone.

Apparently two allergy pills have the same effect as two Vodka gimlets on my ass. I will not be operating heavy machinery.

I can't be sure, but I think there's a blue cardinal at my bird feeder. #Iamthebirdwhisperer

I'm beginning to resent the birds and squirrels for their entitlement issues via the feeder.

Tomorrow is the one week anniversary of my 30th birthday. In lieu of cards and gifts, just send cash.

So as you can see, unless I add in a cupcake competition with midgets and choreographed dance numbers, I don't think I'll be getting my own show any time soon. But I'm okay with that, seeing as it would probably involve makeup and interrupt my standing Friday night date at the grocery store.

Plus, dozens would be lost without my minimal presence on "The Twitter" and updates on small woodland creatures treating my fountain like a day spa.

What can I say (in 140 characters or less)?

I have no shame.

UNCLE JUNE

I would like to introduce you to Uncle June.

As you can see as he poses on my living room table, along with a dirty nose and a slightly vacant look in his eyes, Uncle June also has his suitcase. Why, you might ask? Because Uncle June keeps me company whenever I have to travel for work. My mom and I have a little "gnome" thing we do back and forth, and he's become somewhat of a trip and blog regular.

In fact, Uncle June has been to Orlando, Las Vegas *(he was quite hard to handle on The Strip,)* Houston three times, Dallas, New York a couple of times *(he enjoys Central Park,)* on a Dune Buggy expedition and even to Tennessee *(I took his picture on my balcony with the mountains as a background—he's a trooper.)*

He has been my little touchstone when the plane takes off—the worst part for me—and my dining companion through countless expensed meals. Because while most people feel funny dining alone, I have no reservations placing a three-inch gnome across the booth from me in a fine dining restaurant or café and taking his picture.

When I was in New York, people saw me positioning him "just so" in Times Square and volunteered to take our picture together. It was nice, in a creepy "I'm posing with a little gnome" sort of way.

So, yes, Uncle June has been quite the traveling buddy the past few years and you'll find him scattered through my blog in random posts, some even dedicated to his adventures. After all, it can't hurt to have a little piece of home in a gnome secure in my carry-on, now can it?

I think not.

BUG OFF

I'm basically solar powered, so when it's nice outside, I'm either walking, working out in the yard or basking in the sun like a lizard on a heated rock.

And much like that amphibious analogy, I occasionally eat bugs—or they go up my nose. Not on purpose, mind you, but as an indirect result of talking or breathing while I do the aforementioned activities. Considering one of those things is rather necessary to survival *(although I would argue that both of them are,)* it really can't be avoided.

Just because it can't be avoided doesn't mean it doesn't still tick me off.

Although I know they serve a purpose, bugs suck—both literally and figuratively. Aside from flying up our noses or sneaking in our mouths, they suck the fun out of outdoor situations by sucking the blood out of our innocent souls, leaving us with un-itchable itchy bumps as a reminder of their intrusive visits to our flesh and our fun.

We use sprays, creams, zappers and Tiki torches with citronella oil in an effort to ward off their presence, yet we will still find ourselves cursing the little assholes as we scratch and claw at our bites.

These bugs have balls.

They have no fear.

They laugh at us as we wave our arms around like crazy people and run around the yard with a 75-cent plastic fly swatter that's about as effective as hitting a softball with a wet noodle.

But I refuse to let them win.

They will not stop me from a) breathing or b) talking, therefore running the risk of accidental consumption or a vacuuming up the nose.

I might not have balls and I might have irrational fears of weird things like sneezing while driving or developing an allergy to asparagus, but I'm going to keep doing what I'm doing—lighting torches and swatting at the little bastards, all the while reeking of DEET and frustration.

You've been warned, my flying friends, you've been warned.

WAX ON, WAX OFF

Why I feel I can trust someone with eyebrows drawn in with a pencil to apply hot wax to my face and rip my own eyebrows out, I have no idea. But I do, and it always makes me feel better.

While having it done, I always feel like I'm on some sort of hidden camera show where they laugh at naïve Americans in nail salons. The moment I walk in a smattering of Vietnamese carries throughout the salon and She will appear with a disgusted shake of her head and an, "Ugh. You here for eyebrow wax."

This is not a question, but rather a statement that makes me feel as if I am there to club baby seals instead of simply shape my brows.

We walk past dozens of Buddha sculptures of every shape and size and back to the chair, an American soap opera playing in the background and the smell of strong fumes in the air.

They will continue to talk amongst themselves, and there is usually laughing at some point, causing me to wonder whether I should join in and pretend like I know what they're saying or give her a "look" like I know what they're saying *(about me)* and don't find it amusing.

Considering she will soon be approaching my eyes with hot wax and sharp objects, I remain silent.

"How you?" she asks, and before waiting for an answer she will follow with, "Why you wait so long?"

I'm not a hairy person by any stretch of the imagination, but I've come to realize that anything less than a daily visit will be met with pursed lips and a raised penciled-in brow.

So while she is applying the hot wax to my brows, her face close enough for me to smell garlic and Aqua Net, I tell her I've been busy or give some other excuse that will a) not distract her from the job at hand and b) not cause her to talk to me while her face is that close.

She will cluck her tongue and give me a disapproving look. But this look will be replaced by a smile as she happily rip pieces of cloth from my skin, stripping brow hair and a little piece of my soul while continuing the conversation with the others that I'm convinced revolves around my facial hair and lack of bedazzled fingernails.

She follows up with tweezers, a bit of lotion and smug look of satisfaction—an artist admiring her work. A mirror will be placed approximately two inches from my face for approximately two seconds and I am asked, "You like?"

Again, this is not a question, but rather a statement. Given the fact that she's never given me either the time or reason to dispute that fact, I will nod my head enthusiastically and throw out an overzealous "Always!" or "Looks good!"*

*I blame my giddiness on the chemical cloud hovering over the stations.

We walk past the Buddhas to the front counter, at which point I assume their continuous chatter has now switched over to discussing my tipping habits and how I am about to walk out in public with bright red skin above my eyes.

As I hand her the money, she will tilt her head to the side and point to my hideous nails with a perfectly manicured one of her own. It will be declared that I "need manicure," a statement only slightly less obvious than the fact that the sky is blue.

I fear if I ever exposed her to my feet she would suggest amputation before a pedicure.

But I will not be guilted into additional spa procedures with "Why you no like?" and the eyes of a dozen plastic enlightened spiritual leaders staring at me. She will cluck her tongue and give me a disapproving look, but shrug and move on to her next client waiting in the lobby.

"Ugh. You here for moustache wax," I hear her say as I head for the door and the chatter starts up once again.

Feeling lighter in brows and in spirit, I walk out confident that they're no longer talking about me.

This time.

MY INTERNAL GPS IS MIA

It's not only possible, but 111 percent probable that if you dropped me into any area within a 20-mile radius of my house and gave me directions using only North, East, South and West, I would end up somewhere 40 miles away from my house.

A compass is as foreign to me as self-editing and maps are simply pretty pictures with lots of distracting colors that are entirely impossible to a) understand b) look at while driving and c) fold back up.

In other words, I have no sense of direction.

It's not that I haven't made a valiant effort to understand directions—I'm aware that North, East, South and West exist—it's just that I don't quite understand where they are in relation to where I am or want to be.

In my world, local highways are not labeled by specific names—1-96, I94—but are instead known as the "mall highway," "health food store highway," "work road" etc. Sometimes people that don't know me very well will ask me for directions and in turn get a series of landmarks and things like, "Turn left at the gas station that has my favorite gum that everyone else stopped carrying" as a response.

Not many people ask me for directions after that first time, but I actually feel much worse for people trying to give me directions somewhere.

Here's how a typical conversation with me generally goes:

Other person: Go east on that road about five miles.

Me: Is east left or right?

or

Other person: Head north on that street.

Me: If we're standing in my driveway, is that behind me or in front of me?

In my head I see a flat map with north at the top, south at the bottom and the other two things on the sides. How this translates into real life is somewhat more complicated. Until someone paints a big N, E, S or W in the sky, I'm pretty much screwed.

But I really don't get lost that often, as I end up figuring out my own system—and don't generally travel alone if it's outside that 20 mile radius from my house. If I'm traveling with someone who expects me to be a dependable co-pilot, they soon learn the error of assumption *(and which gas station has my favorite gum that everyone else stopped carrying.)*

I've tried to fix this little issue, but my internal GPS is completely MIA. However, instead of lamenting this directional deficiency of mine, I've embraced it.

I've accepted the fact that I might not always know where I'm going—either in my car, on foot or in life—and that it's OK to stop and ask for directions, even if those directions don't help me out that much at the time.

Even if I take a few wrong turns and feel a bit lost, I take a small amount of comfort in knowing that I seem to find my way eventually.

Just don't ask me how I plan to get there.

I'm still figuring that out myself.

FORECAST: SUNNY WITH A CHANCE OF JAZZ HANDS

There's no polite way to say this, so I'll just come out with it. I've developed unnatural annoyance towards the local weatherman. Let me explain the rationale I use to help me make this seem okay:

Forecast: Obnoxiously Sunny Disposition

While I'm all for enthusiasm, he is entirely too excited about his job — and natural disasters — and wants everyone else to be too. Whether he's stuck outside in a blizzard with icicles forming from his snotty nose or simply flashing his jazz hands in front of a green screen, he's entirely too spastic. A raindrop falls, graphs are drawn and excited overanalysis begins.

Forecast: Flood of Hyperbole

He completely abuses his "Severe Weather" and "Breaking News" privileges.

Yes, we get severe weather, but not every day. His hyperbole and penchant for overexcitement and exaggeration—actually using the phrase "Snowpacolypse" on multiple occasions —have left me indifferent to possible natural disasters. Until I hear sirens and a cow flies by my window, I will assume he's simply meteorologically manic. Again.

Forecast: Cloudy Credibility

I understand he's trying to predict the future, but he's wrong quite often. In an effort to gain credibility, he will tell you to take an umbrella if it's raining and wear a warm coat when it snows. We will then be inundated with station promos about how they "brought us the most accurate forecast" in the area. My suggestion would be to focus on the forecast for 10 minutes from now, not 10 days, and stay humble. You don't get bonus points for doing your job.

Forecast: Slightly Corny

I often feel like I'm watching bad stand-up and the annoying "filler" banter back and forth with the anchor borders on adolescent awkwardness. Weather puns will be made. He will call her by some abbreviated form of her name and "Suze" will politely laugh while looking directly into the camera instead of at him. If it's nice out, she'll thank him for the nice day, to which he will reply, "You're welcome", as if he had control of it. They will laugh and laugh and laugh...

Forecast: Condescension, not to be confused with condensation

Finally—and most importantly—he makes me feel like a social reject with absolutely no life *(on this he's only halfway right—as usual.)* Every forecast is prefaced with something along the lines of, "If you're getting ready to go out to dinner tonight" or "If you're planning a picnic followed by a long walk on the beach tomorrow" etc. Never does he say, "If you're planning on sitting on your couch in your yoga pants watching the ball game and writing a blog post while trying to find that piece of food you just dropped down your shirt," plan on partly sunny skies.

Extended Forecast

Even with all that said, I still watch the weather, mostly because the weatherman has convinced me that I need to find out how the weather won't be when I'm sitting on my couch in yoga pants watching the ball game and writing a blog post while trying to find that piece of food I just dropped down my shirt.

But I *have* started to switch to the Weather Channel and their "Local on the 8's" instead. I usually don't remember the forecast five minutes after I've watched it, but I know it will run again in 10 minutes and the music is catchy.

And catchy music means there's a strong chance of an impromptu dance party in my living room—with jazz hands, of course.

Abby Heugel

A SUGGESTION TO MY COWORKERS WHO PROCREATE

To: Coworkers who want me to love their children as much as they do

I'm a writer/editor and generally go to work to produce things. In fact, I'm even paid to go to work to produce things. One thing I will never produce is offspring, and no disrespect, but I am not paid to find out exactly what the offspring you produced said that was "so cute" or what they produced while sitting on potty.

I have it written in my contract.

Now don't get me wrong. I enjoy personal interaction with you and other coworkers in minimal doses, and although I would rather have a root canal once a week for the rest of my life than have children, I respect your decision to reproduce. Casual conversation about life outside the office can be lovely, but that's not what we're talking about here.

What we're talking about is when you invade my space and force me to hear stories of possible allergies and prolific artistic talents with macaroni and glue, forcing me to concoct ideas on how I can use office supplies to plot your untimely and mysterious disappearance.

I can block you on Facebook and choose to "leave discussion" or "delete conversation." But this option is not available in real life and any attempt to implement these solutions in the office is apparently frowned upon.

So in the interest of keeping the peace in the office—and resentment and homicidal tendencies to a minimum—I thought I might make a few suggestions to help us move past this:

1. Take off the baby blinders and look for the signs. Perhaps you think I'm interested because I'm looking past your head, pretending to look busy at my computer, breathing deeply *(sighing, not in a creepy panting "What are you wearing?" phone call way)* and occasionally nodding my head politely. I'm not. In all actuality, I tuned out the second the words "kidlet" and "breast pump" were dropped into conversation as you dropped off my mail.

2. Keep pictures to a minimum. If you bring in normal pictures and the situation is casual, I might take a genuine interest in seeing what the little bugger looks like. I do not need them emailed to me from your office account and I do not need to receive a mouse pad with your offspring's picture on it. No one not related to you does, and even your relatives are just being polite.

3. NEVER force me to look at an ultrasound picture, as all embryos look like aliens and freak me the heck out.

4. Understand that when I say I don't want to have children, I really mean I don't want to have children. Please do not look at me as if I just declared I don't want to ever have fun or time to myself again, as for me, having children would amount to never having fun or time to myself again. To put it in parental terms, it would be a permanent "time out" for me.

5. Finally, if you bring your child into the office to show them off, please do not be offended if I don't immediately come running out to make conversation in a high-pitched voice, hold them or pet them. I understand that you're proud of the little mouth breathers, and I'm sure they're lovely, but kids are not my thing. If you bring in a puppy, it's a totally different story.

If we can reach a mutual understanding that my office is a kid-free environment, things will go much smoother in the future. If not, the personalized mouse pad will be used as a dartboard.

Just a suggestion

BACKSEAT DRIVER

When it comes to driving, I would say I'm pretty average.

I've never been in an accident *(insert superstitious knocking on wood here)* and have only had one ticket—the story behind that one a post of its own. I admit I have my moments and we all know that I'm directionally disabled, but I generally drive rather aware of my surroundings.

With that said, I sometimes feel like 98 percent of people shouldn't be allowed to operate a vehicle when it's apparent they can't operate a turn signal.

Maybe I'm getting old and cranky, but lately I find myself wanting to run people off the road if only so I can get out and school them on the fact that there are two lanes for a reason and speed limits are not beginning points for negotiations.

In other words, if patience is a virtue, I am void of vehicular virtue.

So in the interest of keeping my road rage to a minimum, I present to you a few observations and suggestions to anyone driving with their head up their ass.

- If you beep your horn .03 seconds after the light changes green, I can promise I will shut off my car, lay on the hood and feed birds for an hour.

- Pulling out in front of me and then proceeding to go ridiculously slow is not excused by the fact that you have those little family people stickers on the back window of your minivan or a WWJD bumper sticker. WWJD? He would go the speed limit.

- However, pulling out in front of me and then proceeding to go ridiculously slow might be excused by the fact that you have a decal or bumper sticker representing a Detroit sports team or love of animals. Go team and go rescue a cat.

- While I appreciate caution, there is no need to stop completely when making a 90-degree turn where there is no stop sign, stop lights or opposite-direction traffic.

- However, there is a need for me to sing everything from "Dancing Queen," to Rage Against the Machine at the top of my lungs. When it comes to car karaoke I'm sort of a professional, so your stares will only encourage my behavior.

- Pick a lane, not your nose. A car is not an invisibility force field that shields you from the general conventions of society. We can see you pick your nose. I don't know if you lost your keys up there or what and to each their own, but when the intense picking of your honker causes you to forget that green means go, I will honk.

- Finally, if you drive a semi truck, please do not race the semi truck in the lane right next to you, forcing all of us to watch this sad little drama play out. Nobody wins, especially the lines of cars stuck behind you. How's your driving? Slow and reckless at the same time, a driving dichotomy if there ever was one.

And let's not forget a couple things in regards to pedestrians—namely me—as I tend to take a lot of walks in the summer and prefer not to fear for my life.

- If I'm walking and you're driving, honking at me and yelling out your window will not encourage me to wave back. It will encourage me to flip you off, as it will scare the shit out of me.

- On that note, if you're talking on your phone as you roll up and through a stop sign and almost run me over, waving, giggling and mouthing "sorry" does not help. One of these times I might just throw myself onto the hood of your car and create a dramatic scene just to freak you out.

Like I said, I am void of vehicular virtue.

You've been warned.

EVERYTHING MUST GO!

Summer is winding down, which means garage sale season is winding down as well. I don't know how it is where you live, but it seems I can't drive 100 feet without seeing a cardboard sign with an arrow pointing me towards the sale of the century each weekend for crap I don't need.

Before I get into the rest details, let's pause and talk about these garage sale signs.

Two tips:

1. People are driving by, meaning they won't read the paragraph you write in 12 pt. font with a pencil on a piece of cardboard. Use bright colors and the word "Sale." You're not pitching a screenplay. You're selling crap.

2. Make sure you spell things correctly. If I see a sign that says "Hudge Sale" as I did a couple weeks ago, I will assume that a dictionary is not among your offerings and will only stop to edit your sign and judge you.

Let's move on.

If you've never actually put on a garage sale yourself and tried to convince people they need to buy the junk you just don't want, allow me to clue you in as to just how much fun they can be. I conducted a yard sale myself a couple years ago and feel I've recovered enough to talk about my experience.

The Night Before: You stay up late making tiny price tag stickers for all the junk you're hoping people will buy. It's early in the game, so you're psychotically optimistic, calculating the total value of your "inventory" at slightly over $5,000, give or take what you can get for those old curtains that came with the house you found stored in the attic.

6: 30 AM The garage sale is scheduled to begin at 8 a.m., but a woman pounds on your door and tell you she "likes to get an early start." When you walk outside to let her "window shop," you notice that not only is the summer weather unpredictably cold and rainy, but that there are five other cars in your driveway.

6: 35 AM One of those cars is your crazy uncle—a black belt in flea markets, weekend auctions and roaming the beach with a metal detector—who is there to help manage the situation. He immediately lays claim to a yard tool he forgot he gave you last week.

9:30 AM You've sold a few things, but are already annoyed with the fact that everything isn't sold and you're not counting your riches. A shopper offers you a dollar for your lawnmower that is brand new and not for sale.

You ask him to leave.

10 AM You look for your uncle and find him drinking Busch Light in a can and offering extras to shoppers for $1 a piece. He tells you he has sold three beers. At 10 a.m..

Noon: You leave the operation in the hands of your uncle/concession seller and go inside to get some lunch. A stranger knocks on your back door and asks to try on some T-shirts for sale, and another wants to know if you have "weenies to go with the beer."

You ask them to leave.

12:30 PM When you return to the sale, you find your uncle slightly manic because he has sold a shovel, a set of garden tools and a hose for 50 cents each. You tell him that they weren't for sale in the first place. He replies that he wondered why there were no price tags.

You ask him to leave. Of course, he won't.

2 PM A group of college boys will stop by and start trying on some of your clothes in the driveway, conducting their own drag queen fashion show. Your mom will attempt to stuff dollar bills into their bejeweled belts *(priced at 50 cents)* and your uncle will offer them beer.

They are cute. You will not ask them to leave. In fact, you will give them the clothes, a few other items and several pathetic come-hither stares.

2:30 PM You decide things are taking entirely too long and start drastically slashing prices like an overzealous mattress salesman who does his own commercials. In fact, you just start giving stuff away and find that's entirely more fun, especially because it pisses off your crazy neighbor lady who is trying to sell a holographic palm tree for $50.

4 PM You're done. You've given almost everything away. It's hard to know what your take is for the day, because at some point your uncle apparently sold the cash box. However, you find a dollar your mom dropped during the impromptu frat boy fashion show and seek out your uncle, who is digging through your "crap I'm throwing away" pile.

4:05 PM You buy a beer.

4:06 PM You vow never to do this again.

VEGUCATION

Let me set the scene.

I was checking out at the grocery store.

There, the scene is set.

Seeing as I buy large amounts of produce and am in the store a few times a week, I generally know the cashiers—the ones that are ridiculously slow, the ones that will let me slip in expired coupons and the ones that know every produce code by heart. This saves me from having to sigh deeply while I wait for the cashier to flip through the little code book for the four-digit number that I've known for years.

Side note: I don't give them the answer, as then they will never learn, now will they?

But sometimes I drop the ball and haphazardly swing into the shortest line, as I did on this particular visit. My groceries were on the belt and I was digging through my coupon book—yes, I am that person—when the cashier first asked me to identify an item. It was spinach, and considering there are a few varieties of greens to choose from, I didn't think much of it.

Not long after she held up my bag of green beans, examining it like it contained a rare species of flora available only in the den of a unicorn in Oz.

She looked truly puzzled, and the following dialogue was exchanged:

Cashier: "Ummm…what are these things?"

Me *(after taking a second to judge if she was serious or not):* "Those? Those are bananas."

Cashier *(after taking a minute to judge if I was serious or not, and evidently deciding I was):* "No, I don't think so. Bananas are yellow. These things are green."

Me *(still trying to decide if she was serious or not):* "There are green bananas, you know."

Cashier *(sadly…still serious):* "Yeah, but they're bigger. I think these are something else."

Me *(finally realizing she can't differentiate between bananas and green beans…sigh):* "Those are green beans."

Cashier *(looking triumphant):* "I knew bananas couldn't be green!"

I had no witty comeback, and even if I did, I'm pretty sure it would have been lost on her.

All I can say is thank goodness the broccoli had a UPC code or I might have had to explain that it wasn't a watermelon.

I know I'm manic about my food, but I was still surprised that there are people out there who don't know a green bean from a banana. Well, there was at least one person who didn't know a green bean from a banana before she was vegucated.

I do what I can, people. I do what I can.

BEING "PUNCTUAL"

Because my goal in life is to "educate" the masses about all the unimportant things that I find tedious, today we will "discuss" something very "important" that I think we all need to "address."

The "overuse" of quotation marks.

I could go into my abhorrence of exclamation points, but we'll save "that" for another time!

While this is obviously a written medium and you're reading what I write, the overuse of quotation marks is not limited to the "written" word. Oh no, the overuse of "air quotes" is also running rampant.

If you're not familiar with "air quotes," I have included the Wikipedia definition below:

"Air quotes, also called finger quotes, are virtual quotation marks formed in the air with one's fingers when speaking. This is typically done with hands held shoulder-width apart and at the eye level of the speaker, with the index and middle fingers on each hand flexing at the beginning and end of the phrase being quoted. The air-quoted phrase is generally very short—a few words at most—in common usage, though sometimes much longer phrases may be used for comedic effect."

What they don't say is that the use of air quotes is generally done in a "sarcastic" manner, a way to "attempt" grammatical justification of a jab.

"So, I hear that you're a writer" has a much different tone than, "So, I hear that you're a 'writer.'"

The first statement has a fairly neutral tone, at least until I add in a few dashes of skepticism and judgment that probably weren't intended but that I implied. However, the second one seems to imply that being a "writer" is a "dubious" distinction.

Side note: *That may very well be the case, but I'm not picking on writers. Feel free to sub in "singer," "actress" or any other profession that I have no talent for doing and that would require the use of sarcastic and judgmental air quotes.*

At any rate, the proliferation of air quotes and quotation marks in general got me "thinking," and I tweeted that after educating the masses about all the unimportant things that I find tedious and eating a meal without spilling on myself, my new goal in life is to find a way to have "air parentheses" and "other" forms of punctuation catch on the way "air quotes" have.

Why do quotes get all the love?

- It's hard to describe "air parentheses," but just imagine that every time you wanted to set off a list or include an aside *(as I am often prone to doing,)* you made big curving arcs with your arms.

- In case your tone makes, "You're pregnant" indistinguishable from "You're pregnant?" you could take one arm and act out the curvy part of a question mark like in a sassy "talk to the hand"-type gesture, accenting it with a punch at the bottom.

- A friend suggested that "air ellipses" could be like repeated poking of the air with index fingers on either side and another added using "air commas" to emphasize your need to pause between phrases and clauses. For this one, I'm envisioning a parade/beauty queen scooping-type wave.

- "Air colons" would be acted out like a boxer's one-two punch, a quick jab-jab to let people know you're starting a list or an explanation that is preceded by a clause that can stand by itself.

- We wouldn't have to worry about the "air semicolon," as no one knows how to use those anyway.

So even though most of you are only subject to "reading" my words and punctuation—and I can promise that exclamation points will always be used minimally!—if you see me in person, feel free to implement "air punctuation."

Because while I find the overuse of "air quotes" rather tedious, I'm totally looking forward to someone trying to implement the "air ampersand."

DON'T SWEAT IT

I've belonged to the same gym for more than 14 years, worked there through college and have frequented numerous other facilities. I've seen a lot, and with a few exceptions, the same people magically appear in any gym on planet Earth. Some of them work out hard, some don't work out at all, and some do exercises so bizarre that it's clearly not safe to be within a 50-foot radius of them.

So I figured I would share a few *new* rules I would implement if I ever owned a gym.

Dress Code

Any gym is a fashion freak show. There will teenage boys in too-big tank-tops and old men in sweatpants, people in jeans trying to ride stationary bikes and "bodybuilders" who consciously decide to wear Hammer pants and fanny packs paired stylishly with weight belts and wrestling shoes.

Women will primp and proceed to work out just hard enough to appear dedicated, but not hard enough to actually break a sweat and appear "glistening."

While annoying, these things do not affect me, as I will continue to look relatively normal in my T-shirt and no makeup in comparison. However, certain things will not be allowed:

- No shirt, no shoes, no sweat, meaning do not wear flip-flops or take off your shoes or shirt. No one wants to see feet, and the germ factor is enough for me to have a panic attack. In addition, men are not allowed to take off their "lifting tank" to admire the results of the eight reps of awesomeness they just did and will record in their little notebook after each set.

- Whether you are male or female, short shorts are not allowed on the inner/outer thigh machine for obvious reasons.

- In general, dudes in the weight room wearing shorts so short and tight that they would be considered in bad taste at a Gay Mardi Gras parade will not be tolerated.

Smells

- If you marinate in perfume or cologne, you will be asked to leave.

- There will be no intentional farting in the gym. Those who do it often explain to those less publically flatulent that it's inevitable when working out so hard and eating large amounts of protein. This is bullshit and it stinks. Literally. Go in the bathroom and return upon release.

Noises

- Outbursts and primal grunting from the "big boys" are often encouraged with statements like, "You got this!" "Lift that shit!" and "It's all you!" from spotters. While I cannot ban this motivational technique, I will ask you to tone it down, if only because I feel embarrassed for you.

- If someone is in the middle of an exercise, do not ask them a question, especially if it's completely unrelated or irrelevant. And it's always unrelated or irrelevant.

- Keep the cell phones in the locker room, as no one need to find out all about how "Treadmill Dude" totally hooked up with that chick from the bar or how "Treadmill Dudette" refuses to call that asshole until he changes his Facebook relationship status from "It's Complicated."

Equipment Use

- The weights have homes. They like their homes. All the little dumbbells go together and all the big ones go together. Two 30 lb dumbbells belong together and every time one gets placed in the spot of the 15 lb dumbbell, God kills a kitten.

- You are not the king/queen of the Cardio Room remote control, especially if you are using a piece of cardio equipment like a sofa and not actually exercising. You obviously do not understand "exercising," and therefore do not deserve the remote control.

- Wet machines should only be the result of sanitizing spray.

- Do not do martial arts in the middle of the gym floor (kicking/punching the air) with your crazy ninja breathing and take up tons of space. Be courteous.

No Stalking

There will be no stalkers, either in or outside of the gym.

- Do not hover around and wait for a piece of equipment or cardio machine despite the fact that there are a plethora of other options you could be using.

- Do not stalk someone for a closer parking spot. You are at a gym, a place most normal people go to exercise, so waiting around for a closer parking spot instead of walking an additional 20 feet makes you look like a douche.

But then again, maybe that's just the fanny pack.

YOU'RE A WEIRDO, BUT THAT'S OKAY

Hey, you.

Yeah, you.

Come in a little closer, closer…

Good.

I want to tell you something very important, something I think you should—no, something I think you *need* to hear.

I just want to tell you that you're not alone,

in feeling the way that you do.

You might be a weirdo for dozens of things,

but never for just being you.

I know, I know…

You're rolling your eyes and sighing out loud,

ready to click of this site.

Letting that guard down is not quite your style,

and talking about it's not right.

But I bet you've had doubt, I bet you've had fear,

I bet that you've questioned your thinking.

Walking that line between okay and not,

feeling your heavy heart sinking.

Days when you feel like the silence you hear,

from words that the others don't say,

is a chasm to fill with assumptions and doubts

about how you have failed in some way.

It might help to know that you're not by yourself,

and that someone else feels that way too,

But maybe they don't know just what they should say,

as they're not as open as you.

Most people won't tell you about all the times,

they feel cheated or hurt or confused.

The might never speak of the ache that they feel

when their confident ego gets bruised.

It's often believed being strong has to mean,

going alone on that ride.

But a stronger thing still is to make yourself fragile,

and speak of those things that you hide.

I bet there are times when you read through a post

and think, "I feel the same exact way."

Relief in the knowledge that someone out there

expresses the words you can't say.

I know this is true as I see it a lot,

in the comments I read here and there.

How someone knocks down any walls that they built

through the words that they've chosen to share.

They might feel a vulnerable itch as they write,

not knowing how things will turn out.

But even if one person kind of relates,

it's enough to erase any doubt.

The person who gets it might not be the one,

that you talk with in person each day.

It might be a "stranger" from some other state,

that takes time to read things you say.

The distance won't matter when matched against depth,

and authentic relationships form.

As shedding the layers of doubt that we wear,

reveals there is no baseline or norm.

My point is that often we feel like we're weird,

and honestly, that's probably true.

But it's not for the reasons we probably think,

It's never for being just you.

Now feel free to click off this site if you must,

I know that his poem's kind of lame.

But sometimes you need a swift kick in the ass,

and *this* weirdo is eager and game.

AT THE CARWASH

I've made no secret of my driving pet peeves, but one of the things I find most difficult about operating a motor vehicle is the car wash. In fact, at times I find it down-right scary.

First of all, I am slightly claustrophobic. Second, I had an unfortunate car wash incident in my childhood that involved our car getting stuck on the track with the headlights of another vehicle quickly approaching while I freaked out and my mom looked at me with her, "I can't believe you're my daughter" face.

You know the one.

Anyway, it starts with the Herculean task of lining my driver's side wheels up with the tiny track line that leads into the car wash cave. I carefully watch the attendant for direction—he waves me a little to the left, to the right, no! no! back to the left!—before I finally receive his seal of approval, a raising of his hand and a stern nod of his head.

I quickly exhale and regroup before remembering I have to put it in neutral and take my hands off the wheel and my foot of the brake . This poses dual problems for yours truly, as first I am worried that I will somehow run over the attendant as he does the initial rising off of my car.

This has never been an issue in the past, but yet I have this concern.

Once I am confident I will not be dragging said attendant under my car throughout the rest of the rinse, I am expected to believe that even though I can't see what's on the other side of the soapy brushes and gushing water, both me and my vehicle are safe.

51

Evidence would suggest otherwise, as after the initial rinse, the big red things that look like giant bottle cleaners come flying at my vehicle in all their whirling glory. At this point I'm still doing fairly well, considering I'm in a car wash, and comforted by the fact that I like clean cars.

But then the blue things start flying at the sides of my car with such force that my external rearview mirror is shoved forward. Considering I have no control over where I'm going and can't see through the suds anyway, this really shouldn't be an issue. However, given my OCD, I have to resist the urge to roll down my window and pull it back into its rightful position.

I stay strong. I resist.

However, at this point I'm begin to freak out a little more because now I've got the big red things flying at my windshield, the big blue things flying at both sides of my car and long linguini-like rags slapping at the roof. I'm convinced that I will be the exception, that they will bust right through my windshield and suffocate me in their sudsy stealth.

So despite the fact that nothing except static will come through in the car wash cave, I blast the radio as loud as I can. I think this is somehow supposed to comfort me.

It doesn't, but planning what I will say to the news reporters who will interview me after my harrowing experience does distract me until the rinse cycle begins.

Around this time I can breathe a little easier, although now I am granted full visual access to my surroundings. This means that the off-kilter mirror is in full view—*I still resist*—as are any cars approaching me from behind on the track.

Giant dryers threaten to suck me into the car wash cave vortex, but I exhale as I literally see the light at the end of the tunnel.

I wait for the blinking red light to turn green so I can perfectly plan the switch from neutral to drive as the track shoves me off. Approximately

2.4 seconds after leaving the car wash cave, I roll down my window and adjust the mirror, with the sight of my car's clean exterior making the $5 spent all worthwhile.

Until the first damn bug hits my windshield.

But it could be worse—I could be the bug.

CSI: POND/FOUNTAIN THING

For the past couple of weeks I have been enjoying the soothing sounds of a gentle waterfall. No, I have not neglected to fix my runny toilet once again, but rather I speak of the fountain/pond in my backyard oasis.

We—*and by "we" I mean my mom*—got it running once again with the help of a new pump and some elbow grease, and the gentle tinkling of the streaming water has been providing a relaxing background as I swat off the bugs of summer.

Well, that went down the crapper.

Empty Pond

The damn thing sprung a leak—again—and has since emptied itself out to reveal a new spot for annoying white fuzzies and tree debris to congregate. I'm not quite sure why it happened, but I would like to blame something other than the fact that it simply sprung a leak.

Enter CSI: Pond/Fountain thing and the short list of suspects.

The Diva Chipmunk

When I left for work the other morning, there was a chipmunk frolicking near the crime scene. Due to my excitement at getting to work at 6:30 a.m., I failed to inform him that I was not running a private spa for small woodland creatures. It's possible that if he chose to swim laps with unpedicured nails, the liner of said pond could have been torn.

However, I feel the small woodland creatures enjoyed the pond as much as I did and doubt this was an impulsive act to display disappointment in my failure to supply little fuzzy robes, acorn appetizers and complimentary slippers. I have eliminated all diva chipmunks as suspects.

The Masked Menace

While I have a soft spot for small woodland creatures, I have no such feelings towards large bastard raccoons that destroy my birdfeeder and refuse to fear me.

The first time I looked out my window and saw this thing climbing up the stairs, I thought it was a bear. *(Never mind the fact that we don't really have bears in my area.)* This beast is huge, and when I ran out flailing my arms and making crazy sounds, it simply moved one step lower and looked positively bored. I swear I heard it sigh before slowly retreating, only to return the second I went back into the house.

So while I would love to nail this sucker to the wall for the crime in question, considering there is no food involved, I don't think it would have the motivation—other than to piss me off.

Ernie the Gnome

With Ernie, jealousy could most certainly be motive. Uncle June—my traveling pocket-sized gnome—get a fair amount of mini-face time on the blog, whereas Ernie only appears in warm-weather situations.

It's very possible that these feelings of inferiority could have manifested themselves into a vindictive act of vandalism, but alas, he would have been destroying his own little humble abode. I feel he must be eliminated from the suspect list as well—along with the turtle.

Long Shots

I thought about blaming the neighbor kids, seeing as they have been wandering around the neighborhood with their improvised nunchucks and potent pellet guns. But they haven't really ventured into my yard since I moved in, at which point in time the little mouth breathers rode their bikes across my front lawn and dug holes in my backyard because the old owners apparently allowed that.

I calmly told them that I didn't allow that behavior and was not above installing an invisible electric fence to prevent a repeat occurrence. I then added that both Santa Claus and the Tooth Fairy had died tragic deaths as a result of their reckless excavation and bicycle operation through my yard.

With that said, they now call me "Miss Abby" and only come over when selling overpriced products for various Scout troops and cults they belong to.

So they've also been eliminated as suspects, leaving me right back where I started from—an empty pond and empty leads. But this investigation has not been for naught, as I'm thinking the neighbor kids might be included as possible allies in the war against the raccoon.

Let's put those nunchucks and pellet guns to good use, shall we?

VELCRO ROLLERS, EYELASH ASS

The other day I Tweeted:

"Just in case anyone wants to live vicariously (and glamorously) through me, I've been at work an hour and just noticed I left a Velcro roller in my hair."

On the bright side, I'm the first one in the office and by myself for at least an hour before anyone else comes in, so no one was witness to my beauty brilliance. On the dark side, I still felt the need to let everyone know what an ass I am.

But this isn't the first time that I've done that, and it got me thinking about how I am a perpetual "Before" picture when it comes to day-to-day beauty.

If someone were to sweep me away and completely make me over, I wouldn't object one perfectly separated eyelash. However, I have no interest in investing either the time or the money in learning how to do it myself—kind of like automotive repair or computer programming, but with more glitter and possibly more power tools.

So while I am *(obsessively)* clean, always smell *(relatively)* lovely, occasionally color my hair and get my eyebrows waxed, my general "beauty" routine consists of washing my hair, putting on a coat of foundation in the winter, mascara, a little eyeliner and lip balm.

That sounds simple enough, but there are even snags with those simple steps:

- When I wash my hair, there have been times I've forgotten to rinse out the conditioner, as I was too distracted reading the back of the bottle in each of the foreign languages.

- And while I start out with styling products and Velcro rollers in the morning, by the afternoon I've usually resigned myself to the fact that my hair would like to join my chest in remaining flat and lifeless. Bobby pins are inserted—in my hair, not my bra—and I move on.

- I have directly applied foundation to my eyeball, resulting in a beige splotch and searing pain.

- Using an eyelash curler is a daily thing, despite the fact that there have been times more times than I can count when I've pinched the skin near my eye with the damn thing and unleashed a string of profanity that scares my eyelashes straight again.

- I have sneezed immediately after applying a coat of mascara and then forget that I sneezed immediately after applying a coat of mascara—more than once. It's attractive.

- We won't even get into my clothes, but let's just say that I do have my "good" T-shirts/jeans/yoga pants/tennis shoes when I need to be classy.

And it seems whenever I do try and make an effort, I wind up at work with a Velcro roller in my head, resentment over having to wear a real "big girl" bra *(for social convention, not out of necessity)* and chicken tracks under my eyes until I remember to look in the mirror.

Plus, my real goal in life is not to learn how to French manicure, but rather to get through a meal without dropping some morsel of food on my "good" T-shirt or finding the fabric softener sheet in my sleeve before someone else does.

But in an effort to make me feel better, a stunning friend of mine who actually works in the beauty industry shared her latest snafu. It seems she wore her fake *(black)* eyelashes to bed and woke up to find what she thought was a huge black spider on her leg, freaked out and started swatting at it with the ferocity of a home run hitter.

In actuality, it was her fake eyelashes stuck to her ass.

That made me feel a little better, if only for the visual.

SNOWPOCALYPSE

People who actually use the word "snowpocalpyse" should be dragged out back and beaten with a wet noodle. It's not clever, and in fact, it's quite annoying.

These same people most likely shorten the name of things that are already shortened or combine the two names of a couple. I repeat—it's not clever, and in fact, it's quite annoying.

Pardon me if I sound a bit cold—*emotionally, not physically*—but I am in Michigan and they are once again predicting the biggest storm of the season to hit later this week, with around 10-16 inches predicted for the area.

If you live in a state that actually has winter—*and 50 degrees does not count as winter to all you California dreamers that complain about rain*—you expect that snow will be part of the forecast. But whether it's because we're all stuck inside for these cold winter months or because CSI: NY is in reruns and we're bored, people tend to go crazy and get obsessed with the weather *(and use words like "snowpocalypse.")*

Here are several things that will happen:

- Manic meteorologists will spend more time telling you that their station has been tracking the storm longer than anyone else than they will actually spend talking about the storm itself. This is their Super Bowl.

- Even if no snow has fallen yet and it has been discovered that there is a recall on oxygen for the entire planet, the news will still lead off with a "breaking news" bulletin to tell you about the impending snowy doom of the area. And remember, you heard it there first.

- Facebook will become the repository for complaints about it being snowy and having to shovel or about the meteorologists being wrong if the storm does in fact pass by without declaring war against our four-wheel drive.

- There will be multiple jokes about the lack of global warming. None of them will be funny.

- Kids everywhere will be making silent deals with the devil in order to have a snow day, while parents everywhere will be making silent deals with the devil in order to send them off to school.

- People who have lived through multiple winters will still neglect to brush the snow off their car and turn on their lights before proceeding to forget how to drive.

- A majority of people will decide that they have to stock up on toilet paper, bread and shovels and talk about nothing except the snow. In Michigan. In winter.

I'm not saying I like the snow— I don't—but it's expected and inevitable.

(And for all of you who tell me to move to a warmer climate, thank you for the suggestion. That will be feasible as soon as I am discovered as the next "Dear Abby" and given a column and condo in California or swept off my feet by a tropical Romeo. The likelihood of either being less than that of a "snowpacalypse" in hell.)

Anyway, here's my advice:

- Make sure that your car has a full tank of gas and emergency provisions in case you get stuck—boots, gloves, blanket, flask of Vodka—the basics.

- Don't rent a new release from the video store, as you will be required to leave your snow shelter to return it the next day under the threat of a possible late fee.

- Stock up on the essentials you will need to get your through not one, but possibly two *(gasp)* weekdays without going to the store.

- Be prepared to shovel and listen to everyone else complain about having to shovel—usually the same people that complain it's too hot in the summer.

- Remember that despite the current snowy situation, Opening Day for baseball season is just two months away.

That, my friends, warms even my cold little heart.

THAT'S WHERE YOU CAME FROM

It all started with a book.

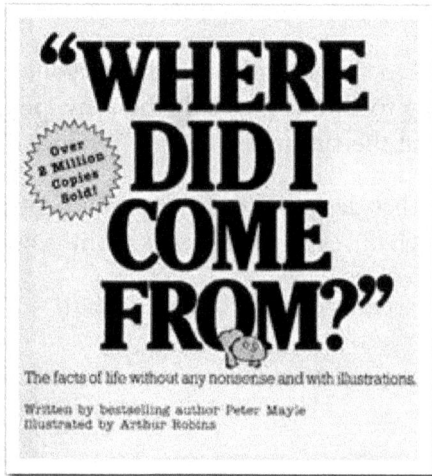

Is it actually how I learned where babies come from?

Of course not, but that doesn't mean it didn't teach me a thing or two about the mechanics. It also doesn't mean that despite the fact that they were cartoon characters, I still wasn't skeptical or mildly horrified.

Up until that point I had a general idea about how things worked but the details were fuzzy, and quite frankly, I liked it that way. When my friend brought the book out, we flipped through it *(many times)* with a mix of curiosity and doubt. There was a lot of skeptical laughter, mostly at the thought of people actually doing that stuff on purpose.

If you're not familiar with the book, it includes cartoon characters in all their naked glory. The image that's burned in my brain is that of the bathtub.

Well, not really the bathtub, but the two overweight naked cartoon adults standing there in all their bare-assed glory. Their smiles and the decorative throw rug in that miniscule bathroom did nothing to distract from the tufts of hair strategically highlighted in lower extremities or the sagging body parts so openly displayed.

These exhibitionists were smiling because they knew they were about to change the lives of children everywhere. With a turning of the page, there was no going back. There was no "unknowing" the things they were about to so happily illustrate through careful word choice and stark illustrations.

This book pulled no punches, and in a clear and concise way it explained exactly what happened when two people "loved each other and wanted to express their love." While it gave you the basics, it left quite a bit out.

Here's the true story.

First of all, most bathtubs are entirely too small for two overweight people, and the book shows him standing up for all to enjoy.

Although we would all be grateful if he actually attempted to sit down in the tub, there would be no room for him. And if by some miracle he squeezes in, there will be no water left. She will be cold, and additionally, she will be pissed because the floor would be flooded.

He will counter with the fact that less water meant more room for lovin' and continue his advances, at which time she will remind him that if there was less of him to "love" and he actually ate the healthy lunches she sent to work with him each day, they might not have this problem.

Knowing he's in a rather vulnerable position, he will gingerly counter with the fact that it's actually *her* taking up the majority of the room in the tub— but that he still wants to fluff those fleshy pillows, if she's in the mood.

She will not be in the mood.

In fact, she will be drying herself off with a towel, muttering about how her mother was probably right and double-checking to make sure she has adequate AA batteries in the nightstand.

He will be left holding the bag, so to speak, but all hope will not be lost. A man on a mission, he will set off to find a mop to rectify the situation. Realizing he doesn't know where they keep the mop—and wisely keeping this information to himself—he will resort to towels.

An hour later, with his attempts to clean the floor complete, he would then proceed to enter the living room where his wife will be on the computer watching back episodes of "The Soup" and feeding her feelings with Fritos.

She will glance up and notice her husband, or rather, she will glance up and notice her husband has created a human towel rack with a certain member of his anatomy.

The ridiculousness of the situation will cause her to unexpectedly laugh.

He will laugh.

The resentment and towel will fall.

And that's where you came from.

PURSES AND PILLOWS AND PUMPKINS, OH MY!

If there's one person who hates shopping for clothes more than me, it's my mom.

The woman will spend hours in Home Depot or a greenhouse, but trying to get her to try on a pair of jeans is like pulling infected teeth out of a rabid badger. I've only been marginally successful in one of those activities, and I still have the scar to prove it.

But the fact is both her purse and her favorite sweatshirt jacket looked as if they had been attacked by a badger. She had a gift card for Kohl's—a gift card she's had for a year—so with the promise of a beer afterwards if she was good, I was able to convince her to go look around.

Considering I need new winter clothes anyway, I figured I could hunt while she sought out the elusive and exotic items on her list that she claimed were impossible to find—jeans, a black purse and a sweatshirt.

We split up, and it took me .8 seconds to remember that I still hate shopping. Clothes in the juniors department said "slutty schoolgirl" while those in the women's department screamed "stodgy schoolmarm."

Considering I wasn't really going for either of those looks *(at that given time, mind you)* I was done looking at clothes five minutes and one stuck-in-this-shirt dressing room experience later.

After wandering around the store and reassuring multiple sales associates that the only thing they could help me find was my mom— they declined, by the way—I texted her to ask her location.

It seems no matter what we do, I always lose her in a store, which is why I do slightly sympathize with parents who take their kids shopping. However, my mom would never agree to be pushed around in a cart or hooked up to one of those leashes, so I'm forced to hunt and seek.

When I did finally find her, I realized she didn't answer my text because she was too busy trying on a sweatshirt jacket over her sweatshirt jacket before claiming it was too small. I tried to convince her to take off her sweatshirt, but I could tell she was also nearing the point where that suggestion was as appealing as badger molar extraction.

You pick your battles.

The good news was that despite not trying on any jeans—they don't carry the one size and style she bought 10 years ago and hasn't been able to find since—she did find a purse. Thank god for small miracles and big bags.

As we went to the checkout, we passed the first sweatshirt jacket we looked at upon entering the store, one dismissed due to some flaw that was now rendered invisible as it was thrown into her cart to take home.

I asked no questions.

Once we checked out and headed for the door, she remembered she wanted to look at pillows, so I agreed to go put our purchases in the truck while she sat on the bench and waited for me to come back.

When I came back approximately 2.3 minutes later, she was not on the bench. I was not surprised.

After wandering around the store and reassuring multiple sales associates that the only thing they could help me find was my mom—they declined, again, a bit more suspiciously—I looked down an aisle and found her lying on the ground trying out a pillow.

The next 10 minutes were spent with her lying on the ground, trying out pillows—unsuccessfully.

So we left and went to buy pumpkins, something much more enjoyable for all involved.

As I was putting them out on my front steps later that night, I got this text from my mom:

> *"Just said a quick prayer over my old purse and buried it while wearing my new sweatshirt and cradling a pumpkin. I kind of feel like a rock star."*

And that, my friends, is considered shopping success.

WHEN THE QUESTION IS THE ANSWER

Here's the thing about Jeopardy.

These people are freaks.

Back when computers were huge monstrosities with only four colors on the screen, I was quite prolific at Jeopardy Jr., Wheel of Fortune, Family Feud and Classic Concentration *(not to mention Oregon Trail and Carmen Sandiego.)*

But in real life?

While I have good days, most of the time when I watch it I get excited if I get at least one or two questions right each round. Half of the time I don't even know what the question is asking. How these people know about countries with a population of three people, two endangered unicorns and several species of rare flora or lines from books written in 1875 is beyond me.

Give me categories that involve food, sports or some type of crafty wordplay and I can occasionally run a category. Once in awhile something from high school science of college French will pop into my head and I'll get a question right.

I will then proceed to celebrate and miss hearing the next three questions/answers.

If by some divine intervention I am able to correctly answer the Final Jeopardy question, I pretty much start filling out applications for Mensa before I realize it's a lot of work and instead go get a snack.

My point is that these people are quite amazing. Even the weirdos that completely blank out and end up getting their name wrong still had to qualify to make it on the show. That is much more than I will ever *(desire to)* do, so props to them. But I do have a suggestion for the contestants:

Work on the interview portion a bit, eh?

Those 30 seconds of awkward "social" interaction with Alex usually cancel out any envy I had for their mental acuity. That might sound harsh, but that time should not be spent sharing that you have an extensive collection of Beanie Babies or that you once found a potato chip that looked like Jesus skiing.

If you have time to memorize the temperature of every star in the solar system, you have time to plan this part out a little better. At least run the idea by your friends and family if only to spare them from fast-forwarding through this part at the watch party you will throw yourself when the show airs.

At least make something up.

You're smart.

BEWARE THE MALL

Today I will use this space to educate the dozens of you that flock here on a monthly basis to skim my posts.

Why? Because the mall can be a dangerous place.

The fact that I don't particularly enjoy shopping for clothes is not a secret. While I enjoy walking around the mall on occasion, the general premise of immersing myself in an environment of consumerism and hormonal teenagers is not exactly my idea of enjoyment—minus the bookstore, of course.

And while I realize that shopping in Michigan pales in comparison to shopping in big cities like L.A. and New York, I thought I would pass along a few of my tips for surviving the mall—a mall PSA of sorts— for those of you who share my sentiments.

- First of all, if you don't have money to spend on anything "extra," you will come across 1,001 things that you actually like and want to buy. If you have a gift card or money to spend, you will find nothing. With that in mind, proceed.

Scent of a Woman

- The perfume counter is a trap. I try and rush through this maze of pink packaging, celebrity endorsement posters and overpowering scents without making eye contact with anyone wearing the minimum 3 lbs of facial makeup, a nametag and a fake smile. They will corner you and spray you with things that you will not be able to scrub off for days.

Gangs

- Beware the teenage girls! They travel in packs and although their behavior is predictable, it can still be a cause of concern. You can spot them by their clothing—either they try entirely too hard or not at all. For example, they will be overdressed in an outfit more appropriate for a dance club than the mall, despite the fact they have never paid for a piece of clothing themselves *(minus the thongs and lacy bras they bought without their parents knowing.)*

- On the other hand, some will feel it's socially acceptable to wear pajama pants—occasionally rolling down the waist to reveal aforementioned thong—and flip-flops. While I'm not fashionista, I would think that if you took the time to put on makeup and the Bump-It in your hair in an effort to impress the dude working in GNC, you could find a pair of pants that you haven't slept in.

* Their male counterparts do not pose such a risk, despite their Bieber-esque façade. They are simply there for the food and the girls, in that order.

Germ Gym

- Filled with things for them to climb on, slide down and fall off of, the children's play area is a breeding ground for everything that will cause you to feel miserable. This can be the result of the loud screaming, both by parents and children, or the fact that every germ from every disease will be crawling around said play area and soon transferred to other shoppers walking by. Avoid this area at all costs.

* However, if you are a parent of the teenage girls above, make them sit there for an hour and observe—best birth control ever.

Technical Difficulties

- Just walking through the mall can be dangerous, not because you might be inclined to trip over your own feet or going up stairs like some people we know, but because of technology.

People will be walking in groups and texting other people in groups, meaning there are numerous groups of people walking around with their heads looking down or stuck up their ass.

- They will not appreciate it when your stubbornness does not allow you to yield to their rudeness, they run directly into you and you snarkily excuse them when they fail to do so themselves. They will scoff, glare and most likely text about what an asshole this person at the mall was.

You can do the same.

Book It

- The bookstore is pretty much a safe environment, although you do have to watch out for paper cuts and falling subscription cards from the magazines you stand there and read for free instead of actually buying. Plus, there is always the danger of spending too much money, but if you have to spend it on something at the mall, you can't go wrong with books.

So I hope you at least learned something from this post so that your time has not been wasted.

If you haven't yet, I will leave you with the fact that a Komodo dragon uses its long tongue to pick up smells in the air, zeroing in on rotting meat from more than a mile away.

If you knew that, I got nothing, which is how I came home from my last trip to the mall-except for that paper cut.

POWER TO THE PEOPLE

Alternate title: *Reason No. 873,298 why I'm neurotic*

Whether it's hot or cold, an earthquake or a hurricane, people love to talk about the weather.

Living in Michigan, there's usually a lot to talk about. While we don't get hurricanes, we do have pretty much everything else. Summer days can reach 100 degrees while winters can bring 100 inches of snow, and sometimes the temperature can vary as much as 30-40 degrees from morning to afternoon.

When the fall colors are in full bloom and nature paints an indescribable picture of beauty, I'm grateful for the season. When it's oppressively hot or my 25 min. commute takes an hour in the snow, I'm grateful for Vodka.

My point is that we deal with a lot of weather-related things out of our control, and for the most part, I roll with the meteorological punches by lamenting the fact that Mother Nature hates me and wants me to be unhappy.

However, there is one thing that totally makes me go ape shit and elevates my level of neuroticism to new altitudes—losing power.

Let's get one thing straight—I'm really not high maintenance. But good lord, when the power goes out, all rationality and Zen-like tendencies go right along with it, not to be restored until Consumer's Energy plugs things back in.

And you can be sure I obsessively call Consumer's Energy or check online *(briefly, of course, to conserve energy)* to get a restoration estimate, usually being told it will happen at some point hours or days after I totally lose my shit *(which is, of course, the second that I lose power.)*

Here's the general order of operations:

- The semi-creepy weather rolls in and I get on high alert. Like a hunting dog catching the smell of its prey, my eyes get big, my head jerks up and I immediately assume that rumbles in the distance are an impending weather-related disaster headed directly for my house.

- I will text my mom and ask her if I should be worried. Knowing what a weather weirdo I am, she will usually beat me to the punch with something like, "Chill the hell out. It's just thunder. You'll be fine" or "Can I have your couch if you get swept up in the storm?"

- If I'm at work, all productivity ceases while I play out various scenarios in my head, check radar online and take into account exactly what I have in my fridge/freezer at home, as food waste is my main concern with possible loss of power. If it's winter, I figure I can throw things outside and warm up some food on the stove. If it's summer, I freak out and pack that bitch up like an igloo.

- If I'm at home, everything not related to obsessively watching the weather channel and lighting candles ceases while I play out various scenarios in my head and take into account exactly what I have in my fridge/freezer. If there's Vodka, I rationalize that using a straw is acceptable and than nothing should go to waste.

- Mini-blinds will be shut and the TV will be turned up loud, as to drown out not only the sound of the thunder, but also crazy neighbor lady yelling at her dogs to "go poo-poo" and bitching about how the wind puts her cigarette out. Her Vodka was gone by 7a.m. and she rarely consumes solid food, so that's not a worry for her.

- I will perfectly situate my flashlights and I will wait. I will make promises to unseen higher powers that as long as I don't lose power, I will be fine and work on saving the world in the morning *(a task that would conceivably require electricity, therefore eliminating me from the impending power outage.)*

Of course most of the time nothing happens, as storms will roll through and all will be fine. Plus, things smell delightful given the fact that I've lit every candle in the house. My mom will text me to make sure I'm not in a blankie fort in the basement or curled up in the bathtub and I will tell her how insane her suggestion is while slowly crawling out from under the dining room table.

But those few times a year when I do lose power, when I'm forced to miss the game on TV, am disconnected from the Internet and stress about my perishables in the fridge?

I can predict my own neurotic natural disaster—no power required.

IRONING OUT THE DETAILS

When I bought my house three years ago, I somehow got this idea in my head that I needed to buy an ironing board and an iron. This wasn't predicated by the fact that I had an ironing compulsion or even ironed casually at any time before, so I'm not sure where this came from.

All I knew was that if I needed to iron something, I wouldn't have an iron to accomplish the task. Never mind the fact that I was still in need of a couch or a bed at the time, I felt that before I moved in I needed an iron to prevent a possibly wrinkly situation.

So I bought the stuff and stored it in my linen closet, just in case I accidentally purchased something in the future that had a propensity for wrinkling when thrown in a ball on the floor *(usually a deal breaker when factored into the purchasing decision, but sometimes I am fooled.)*

This was the situation earlier this week when a new pair of freshly washed pants was left in the dryer too long.

Wrinkles.

I was ticked that I had purchased something with such an obvious character flaw—cracking under pressure—but also a little bit excited that I was going to be able to use my ironing supplies for the first time.

Yes, the first time in three years.

So imagine my disappointment when I went to my closet and came out with this.

It might just look like an odd angle or that it's low to the ground, but let me post my shoe next to my ironing board for a size comparison...

...and now with my pants, in all their wrinkled glory.

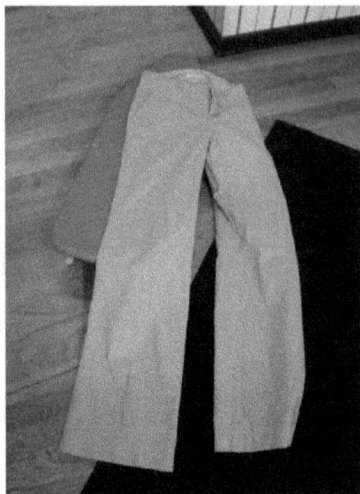

Is it supposed to be that small? I remembered it being much bigger.

While I'm tall, I am not an 8-foot tall Amazon woman with ridiculously long legs, which means this ironing board is better suited for the clothes of Uncle June—my pocket-sized traveling gnome—than for the clothes for yours truly.

But when you have wrinkles and OCD, you have to take action, so I spent a good 15 minutes basically lying on the floor in an attempt to iron a pair of pants on a board two feet too short and elevated approximately two inches from the floor.

I suppose I could have put it on a table, but that would have involved finding an empty space large enough to accommodate the small board. Other than my glass kitchen table, I was kind of screwed.

Not to mention the fact that I thought about that 10 minutes after I had already ironed the pants.

But it was upon completion of this task that I discovered the one truly awesome thing about this ironing board—the absolutely delightful ease at which it collapses. In fact, it collapsed while I was ironing and I didn't even notice.

Maybe I'm just "special," but have you ever succeeded in collapsing a regular ironing board without spewing profanity or getting a random body part stuck in one of the two metal pieces that are somehow more difficult to master than a Mensa test?

Whenever I use a normal ironing board—usually only when I travel for work—I always just leave the damn thing up and use it as a table. Somehow I don't think this would work in my upstairs hallway. Plus, then I would have to dust around it.

The moral of the story is that I should avoid shopping to avoid fighting with inanimate objects so I can avoid writing about diminutively-sized ironing boards and instead sip a cocktail while sitting in the sun listening to the ballgame on the radio.

Well, at least that's what I got out of it.

SWIFFER SINK SAGA OF 2011

Every once in awhile an appliance or fixture in my house decides to call attention to itself and throw some kind of fit. This time it's my sink, as it has decided to drip down below onto the floor of my cupboard.

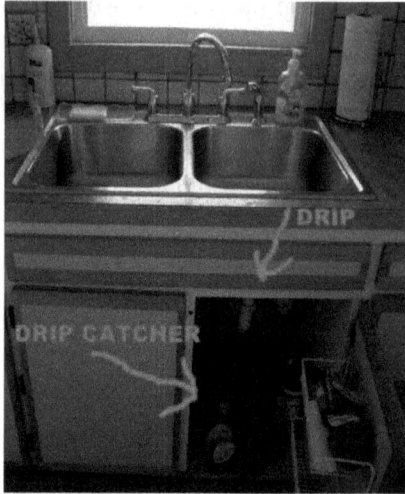

As you can imagine, this did not thrill me.

Any disruption to basic necessities— water, food, Internet, Baseball Tonight, power —are basically classified as mini-catastrophes in my world. If I don't have a sink, how can I make my tea? Use my steamer? Make my lunch for work at that exact second instead of later in the evening? How am I supposed to survive?!?

These were my thoughts about two seconds after this drippy discovery.

I was really trying to go with the flow—*I know life is full of malfunctioning appliances and people*—but when that flow is slowly dripping out under my sink every time I run the water, I tend to spout out my frustration in various forms.

Part of my frustration comes from not being able to fix it myself, but 99.9 percent of my frustration comes from the series of events that follow after my stepdad *(or anyone)* comes over to "fix" it.

*Yes, I am most appreciative, but I am also OCD with no patience for putzing or lack of respect for the Lysol.

So without further putzing, let's take a look at how my Sunday afternoon went (all times are approximate.)

1 pm—It is Swiffer Sunday, so I throw everything into my dining room and proceed to do the Wet Jet waltz across my kitchen. While the floors dry, I go for a walk.

1:30—Get back, wash my hands and reach below the sink for the dish soap, only to discover a small puddle.

1:31—Express puzzlement over said puddle to inanimate objects within earshot and wipe it up with paper towel.

1: 32—Ignore real problem and move on.

2:30—Forget I was going to do the dishes, reach down for dish soap again and rediscover another puddle. Swear under *(and over)* my breath and call my stepdad to express my puzzlement over said puddle.

3:00—Stepdad arrives, does not take his shoes off before entering my Swiffered kitchen floor and going below the sink.

3:00:10—Remind myself he's helping me out and try to ignore that he did not take his shoes off before entering my Swiffered kitchen floor. Deep breaths are taken and possibly exhaled as a loud sigh—this part is sketchy.

3:30—After tearing apart the sink and putting tools on the rug, it is decided he needs to go to Home Depot and I "need to chill out."

Whatever.

3:31—He leaves. A towel is placed under his tools. While placing said towel, I realize the dishes are stacked on the counter—a situation that *(obviously)* needs to be remedied immediately.

3:35—Dishes and dish drainer are transported to the bathtub where they are thoroughly washed. Being crouched at that level, I notice the floor could stand to be vacuumed and heck, while I'm down there, the toilet should be cleaned.

4:00—Stepdad returns with the parts—he thinks—and I continue to stay out of the kitchen, not because I will be in the way, but because I will be tempted to Swiffer stalk him and poo-poo his putzing.

4:01—Plop down on the couch to watch the ballgame, something I had planned on doing before the Swiffer Sink Saga of 2011.

4:20—Try to ignore the clanking tools in the next room, decide I'm pretty much a revolutionary and applaud my survival skills in times of such stress.

4:21—Re-enter the kitchen, see what I declare to be a critical cleaning crisis and immediately change my mind on revolutionary status. However, I am informed it's "fixed" and that he's heading home.

4:25—Air kisses are exchanged, appreciation is heaped upon his ego before the dish drainer is put back in its rightful home, the shower is scrubbed and the Swiffer is put to good use. Again.

5:00—Make food—carefully avoiding the side of the sink that has drying caulk—and plop down on the couch to watch the end of the ballgame. Feel better, as this is your happy place.

Next afternoon—Fill sink, empty sink, discover it's still dripping down below. Throw something—a tantrum or a fork—and take a deep breath.

Make a phone call. Make a drink.

Call it good.

FARMERS MARK-ETIQUETTE

This past weekend I went to the Farmer's Market for what will probably be the last time this year, as Michigan tends to get cold and nasty in the blink of an eye.

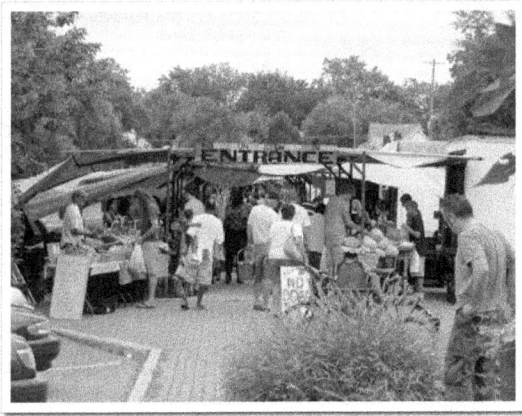

Since I'm still in the "denial" stage of the temporary end of this relationship, I figured I would write a post about our courtship before I progress to the anger and mourning stages of this transition.

Actually, this post was sparked by a few things I observed and overheard the last time I went, so thank you to the douche canoes that neglected to use what I consider Farmer's Mark-etiquette.

Let's begin.

Most markets bring in an eclectic mix of people—everything from yuppies with their soy half-calf sugar-free oxygen enriched lattes and hippie types with their messy ponytails and fair trade sandals made of bamboo bark to families and people like me—most often clad in yoga pants with my reusable tote, ready to knock over the elderly and small children for the perfect loaf of mini pumpkin bread.

In other words, it's a bit of a market melting pot.

There are a couple of rules that are spelled out on signs, one of them being "no dogs" in the actual market area due to the close quarters.

This doesn't stop people from stuffing the little ones in bags and sneaking them in, a sight that continues to amuse me on an almost publically unacceptable level.

There are also rules that aren't spelled out, perhaps assumed as common sense. However, if you've ever talked to another human anywhere, you know there should be no assumptions when it comes to common sense.

So if I were deemed the Market Queen for a Day—a position I anoint myself with in my head every time that I go—here are the rules I would post:

- They are samples people, this is not a buffet. Take one or two and move on.

- Dogs might not be allowed, but children are. With that said, strollers that are three-wide and plow through like a semi need to be banned. Also, it is not cute when your child who is just learning to walk is staggering down the center of a busy aisle at the pace of a turtle, causing people to run into each other, possibly smashing delicate produce and toes.

- Bring your own bags, if possible, as carrying around 12 plastic bags while touting your earth-friendly awesomeness paints a picture of confusion.

May I suggest you do not say the following things:

- These carrots/radishes/etc. have dirt on them!

- Do you have change for $100 bill?

- If I buy two pounds at $2/lb, can I get a discount?

- Were these parsnips humanely killed?

- It's cheaper at Wal-Mart.

- How come you never have fries or creamed corn?

- Do you use the good pesticides?

- How much for just one?

While breaking any of these Farmers Mark-etiquette rules is not a punishable crime, it wouldn't be unreasonable to think that other market goers might harbor inclinations to beat you senseless with a preservative-free baguette or sharpen their aim with a fresh arsenal of golf ball-sized (dirty) radishes.

And as Market Queen for a day—at least in my own head—I can't promise I won't join them.

FALSE ADVERTISING

Anticipation. Cut into an avocado and it was 50 percent pit. Disappointment. I totally know how guys feel when encountering a padded bra.

This post was in response to a writing prompt to write a story as a Tweet with 140 characters or less.

PART 2: FROM WHAT I CAN RECALL

"Isn't the past what people remember—who did what, how and why? And what people remember, isn't that mostly what they've already chosen to believe?" –Amy Tan, "The Opposite of Fate"

My life has had its share of ups, downs and plenty of sideways train wrecks. There have been great people and questionable characters, both contributing to my neuroticism in some significant way. I always thought that if I could get myself to form a sentence about them, it would be one heck of a memoir.

But because I have the attention span of a gnat with ADD, I decided to just write random blog posts about certain things I think I remember about growing up and my family. If I had to estimate, I would say these stories are 93 percent accurate, with the other 7 percent lost as a result of falling off my first two-wheeler and into my mom's rosebushes.

I've blocked out that time in my life.

At any rate, this a bit more about me.

DEAR TOOTH FAIRY: MOVE YOUR ASS

A text I got from my mom last night might give you a bit of insight into my early command of authority:

> *"I was cleaning out some drawers of mine and found a note you wrote the Tooth Fairy. OMG. You were so direct and authoritative. Made me laugh. Then cry. Thank you for being a wonderful weirdo."*

I had to investigate.

On a little 3-by-3-inch piece of paper was the following, word for word, scratched out in pencil:

Dear Tooth Fairy,

Hello again.

You need to know that this tooth was really a pin in the butt! I could twist it all the way around!! It was a lot of work!!!

Please leave the money under my pillow and sign your name on the line below:

*X*_____

The pencil is on my desk. Please don't use my purple pen. It's my favorite.

Have a good night!

Let's "workshop" this, shall we?

I like how I conveyed a sense of familiarity with the addition of "again" to my "hello." Then I get right to the point, telling her the necessary information surrounding the situation and the effort I had put forth to extract said tooth.

I also think it was a nice touch the way I built up the emotion with progressively more exclamation points each time.

Then I rounded things out with the call to action and verification of her status —money under pillow, sign on the line, avoid purple pen— to clear up any confusion, before politely wishing her well on the remainder of her rounds.

Yes, I am a wonderful weirdo.

BUS 315

Sun tan accentuated by pastel dress, white socks, charm bracelet and mullet for me?

Check.

Polo shirt, navy corduroys and R2D3/C3PO backpack for him?

Check.

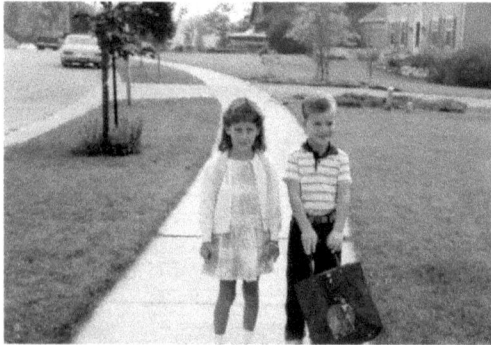

Two nervous moms seeing their whirling dervishes off to the bus stop for the first day of kindergarten, secretly glad to have them out of their hair after a summer of knock-down drag-out kickball games, Barbie mutilations and Double Dare in the front yard?

Check.

My best friend and I were off, but school wasn't the first thing on our minds as we made our way down the sidewalk. What we were really looking forward to, what we had heard so much about from the older kids, was the bus stop and the ride to school.

All the fun happened at the bus stop down the road, which was actually the driveway of two neighborhood kids who assigned themselves entirely too much importance based on that fact.

At the bus stop, backpacks full of Trapper Keepers, sack lunches and permission slips were thrown to the side so the fun could begin. A dozen of us would play Mother May I?, Red Light, Green Light or dodge ball, often getting our clothes dirty before we even set foot on the bus.

When the bus did finally show up—bus 315—Mrs. Hooper would greet us with a smile, something she did every morning of my elementary school career. She was intimidating that first day—a large older woman with crazy gray hair and sunglasses the size of her head—but she gave us candy.

It wasn't a tough sell.

That first day we learned that the bus was more than just a way to get us to school, but rather a way to build character. There were really no rules on the bus, at least any they could really enforce. Since Mrs. Hooper had to watch the road, she could yell all she wanted, but short of stopping that bus and turning it around, couldn't actually stop anything that went on in the back.

And all the good stuff went on in the back.

Oh yes, the back seating arrangement was a symbol of status where seats were saved and secrets, snacks and homework answers were shared. You learned about drinking or smoking as heard from someone's older brother's friend, gross inside jokes were created and seats were vandalized with markers and colored gel pens.

Stuck up front in those green vinyl seats, we longed to inch our way to the back.

But for those first couple of years, we just went along for the seatbelt-less ride. Even on that first day, it was evident that riding the bus made you tough. You had to get up earlier, stand out in the cold and deal with bus stop bullies. The bus is where the best flavored Lip Smackers were traded and playground strategies were discussed.

If weather or a dentist appointment caused you to be picked up and dropped off one day by your parents, you couldn't help but wonder what you missed that day on the bus, who sat in your seat or racked up the Red Rover points.

But on that first day of school we knew none of those things, we only knew school had begun.

Well, and that we looked like total bad-asses.

SIMPLE MATH

It started with Goldfish crackers.

While the details are fuzzy, I remember that it was sometime in October and that on this particular day it was raining outside—indoor recess.

Stuck to the board was Wilbur—a brown *(felt)* bear the first-grade class dressed each day with weather-appropriate clothes. Sporting a yellow rain slicker, boots and an umbrella under a *(felt)* gray cloud and a handful of raindrops, there was no question as to the conditions outside.

The conditions inside most likely included a fascinating discussion about shapes, colors and the pros and cons of multinationals and globalization in a modern society.

That's not important.

What was important was the seating chart, for the stars were aligned— or grossly misinformed—and my desk at the time was conveniently located in a block of four with two of my best friends, both boys and both my neighbors.

For the sake of their self-proclaimed innocence, let's call them M and D. D was my best, best friend, but I kept M along for the ride—even marrying him once or twice in his basement and often skating sweaty hand in sweaty hand to couple's skate at school skating parties in later years. He served a role.

With the polygamous nature of our playgroup, I think Mike knew and served this role well.

As for the day in question, we were doing some sort of math exercise that involved using Goldfish crackers as counting pieces. The details aren't important, but what is important to note is that D had to leave for weekly speech therapy. His Goldfish crackers, unmanned and vulnerable, would not be joining him.

I was hungry—or I just wanted them, again the details are fuzzy—and the Goldfish were consumed. M wanted in. I obliged.

Two for me, one for M. Two for me, one for M. Two for me, none for M, as our mid-math snack was cut short by the intrusive presence of the authoritative adult that has instigated this cracker caper in the first place. Apparently our behavior was being frowned upon and warranted a lecture.

M cried like a kindergarten baby, blubbering out promises to give our lisping buddy all the Halloween candy he anticipated hoarding in the coming days.

I was stoic, annoyed with both the interruption and the insinuation that I had done something wrong. I knew I should feel bad. The reaction from my teacher, the sobbing fool next to me, and the quiet hush that had fallen over the class were telling me as much.

After all, it was D. It was crackers.

So while the teacher was lecturing the class on what was most likely the importance of sharing and stealing, I was building a solid argument up in my head. I wasn't a criminal. I knew right from wrong, good from bad, snacking from stealing.

There were countless times before and would be countless times in the future when D would take (and eat) things that were mine, when he would participate in some plot against my scheduled script of play, when he would be told to "get off my property" or kick me out of his tree fort. I failed to see the importance of a handful of crackers that could be easily replaced and forgotten.

It was D, dammit. It was crackers.

Emboldened by my rationalizations and oblivious to danger, I looked left. I looked right. I looked down at the remaining fish on D's desk, baiting me as they were with their innocent smiles and bright orange glow.

It started with Goldfish crackers.

It ended with crumbs.

Simple math.

BIRTHDAY HIT LIST

Every year for the past 29 years, there have been cake, presents and decorations for my birthday in some way, shape or form. And after 29 birthdays, there should be one memory that sticks out to me the most, one birthday celebration that took the cake, so to speak, and set all the others to shame.

And yet when I think back throughout the years, it all just blends together into a mosaic of memories with one thing in common—my birthday, the day when I can get away with saying it's truly all about me without sounding like a queen.

Set your calendars.

Because it fell in the summer, my birthday served as an excuse to throw many large parties with copious amounts of friends, my large family and food. The crowds and hoopla gradually stopped as everyone grew up and away—or got tired of me—but the bits and pieces of birthdays gone by will always remain in my mind.

Well, at least until I get senile, and considering I recently found my phone in the fridge, that day could come sooner than planned.

But for now, here are a few of the *(literal)* hits and misses.

Strike One

There was a Fiesta themed party complete with stereotypical sombreros and music, Mexican food and a piñata. While a piñata was good in theory, that theory flew out the window right about the time the piñata stick accidentally flew through the air and directly towards an inattentive neighbor lady.

Smarties and plastic jewelry did not fall out of the cut on her head.

Our disappointment was profound.

Strike Two

Nothing fell out of the cut on my head a few years later when my presents were hid throughout our large backyard and I was blindfolded and forced to hunt for them on my hands and knees. A Frisbee was thrown from a great distance and managed to hit me square in the head. Being blindfolded and covered in grass burns, this was literally a blow to what dignity I had left.

We had cake. I forgave.

Strike Three

Then there was a year that the stars aligned and the Tigers were playing the California Angels at home on my birthday. I was convinced I was going to marry their first baseman—JT Snow. This was obviously a sign of our destined eternal bliss.

We drove the three hours to the game, where after a couple innings he came up to bat and hit a foul ball directly towards my dad.

A great ending to this story would be that he made an effort, caught the ball and concluded the perfect birthday of his 10-year-old daughter. Didn't happen. In fact, he never even reached up to catch the damn ball.

We had cake. I had resentment.

But despite the few *(literal)* hits and misses, I have to say that I've had it pretty good. I don't expect a marriage proposal or physical and emotional scarring this year, but I _do_ expect applause when I enter the room and a tiara to wear.

In other words, treat it just like any other day.

This post was written a few weeks before my 30th birthday. And for the record, I did receive a tiara from my mom to wear for the occasion…and any random weekday.

IT WAS AS DRIVE-BY BEACHING

Today I am going to tell you a story about the time me and my best friend B went away together for Spring Break.

This could conjure up expectations of a "Girls Gone Wild" type post if I failed to omit one important detail—we were 8th grade girls and we went to Florida to stay with my grandparents at their condo.

Every morning we would throw on our suits, flip-flops and tanning accelerator, hop on three-wheeled bicycles and spend our days in the sun by the community pool. Aside from the occasional water aerobics class and shuffleboard tournament, we basically had the place to ourselves.

My grandma was someone who believed that once meat was cooked, it didn't need to be refrigerated and could be left out on the hot countertop until it was either consumed or it disintegrated. What did need to be refrigerated—or more specifically, kept in large Ziploc bags in the freezer—were ketchup and mustard packets from various fast food establishments that always gave out "free condiments."

Because of a desire to avoid food poisoning, we often suggested frequenting various chain restaurants for dinner, be it Gram's favorite—Juicy Lucy—or something more familiar to those of us under the age of 65. This suggestion was often well-received, not only because my grandpa loved to eat anything anywhere, but because Happy Hour drinks were 2-for-1 at most of these restaurants—as long as you ordered both drinks at the same time.

That meant that when you walked into any Applebees, Outback, etc. between the hours of 4-6, you would be greeted with tables full of senior citizens pushing their oxygen tanks off to the side of their booths to make room for their two Rum and Cokes, Screwdrivers or Vodka Tonics.

The waitresses were thrilled with their tips, I'm sure.

One day my grandparents presented us with an exciting proposition—going to the beach. About an hour away, the beach was where the action was. We eagerly packed our beach bags and hopped into the backseat the Cadillac, windows down, Neil Diamond warbling from the speakers.

As we got closer, B and I exchanged excited glances and gathered up our bags, waiting for the car to slow down and park so we could join in the whole beach experience.

The car never stopped.

"This is the beach," said my grandpa, proudly pointing it out as we kept driving by. Confused, I asked where we were going to park.

"What? Why would we?" asked my grandma, looking at me as if I had just suggested only playing 12 Bingo cards at once or actually refrigerating leftover chicken. "It's too busy, too hot. Do you girls want some ice cream?"

Now mortified, I looked at B and saw panic in her eyes. The only way we wanted ice cream was if it could be eaten on the beach, which meant the car would have to stop at some point soon.

But despite my protests, the next time the car stopped was at McDonalds just off the highway. Grandpa placed the order of sundaes and cones while we sat in shock in the back. No basking in the sun on the sand, no dipping our toes in the ocean—just a drive-by in the Caddy and "Sweet Caroline" on repeat.

As we pulled up to the pick-up window, my grandma leaned over the driver's seat and gave strict orders to the window worker to include the condiments, which I naively assumed to be the optional nuts for her sundae.

In retrospect, I should have been prepared to hear her demand not the nuts, but the free packets of ketchup and mustard to add to her collection back home.

"Free condiments means free condiments," she said with a chortle, turning around to face us in the backseat. "When you're paying *(.99 cents)* for each ice cream, you better make sure you get your money's worth."

Because after all, nothing completes a day at the beach like free ketchup and mustard to hoard with your ice cream.

"Now who's ready for happy hour?" she asked, tucking the packets into her oversized purse, no doubt to make room for the sugar sure to be swiped from the restaurant.

I looked at B and saw hope in her eyes.

We were ready.

Make it a double.

VIVE LA FRANCE!

There's just a certain, *je ne sais quoi* about the melodic sing-song nature of the French language.

Let me rephrase that.

There's just a certain, *je ne sais quoi* about the melodic sing-song nature of the French language when spoken by someone who can actually speak the French language.

When you're in high school and studying French as a graduation requirement, the cadence of dialogue resembles a choppy staccato more than a flowing ballad. The words don't exactly ebb and flow in intensity with each inflection, rolling off the tongue like butter from the croissant that students are struggling to remember the gender of as they reenact an awkward café scene in front of their overly enthusiastic French teacher.

For my high school teacher, to teach our class was to teach us about a life she was meant to be living 3,000 miles away.

Madame was convinced she was born in France and not in Michigan, and to prove that she immersed herself in the culture of a country she had visited just twice. This love extended to not just her professional life, but also to a mullet, unshaved legs and children who could speak better French than half of Paris.

As high school students, our first goal was to learn the curse words, how to ask for the bathroom and how to proposition complete strangers to sleep with us. Our second goal was to convince Madame to throw French "rendezvous" with snacks and "French" movies.

Considering her children had the complete collections of both Babar and Madeline and that she took our desire for food as a desire to experience the culture hands-on, we had an alarming number of lessons that more resembled a 2-year-old's birthday party.

The conversation was only marginally more advanced.

We were forced to endure workbook after workbook of conjugation and verbs, describe our mood and the weather with alarming frequency and take an unnatural interest in the lives of manically happy strangers talking on videos and tapes about how where they were going in their blue car on various days of the week.

While I got to the point in my studies where I could read and understand a great deal of French, my spoken attempts remained choppy at best.

Madame, who eventually refused to speak English after two years, would speak to us as if in song. Each inflection lulled me into a false sense of security that the same thing would happen when I opened my mouth and attempted to reply.

Yet when I set out to join her in a duet of dialogue, the words seemed to stick in my throat. More cacophonic than melodic, I struggled in vain to tell her that I was going to the bibliotheque on my bike on Tuesday and that I was happy about the weather.

"Viola! Can I write it down instead?

How about another Babar party?

I'll bring the crepes."

At any rate, I recently ran into Madame at the store. Twelve years later she was still rocking the mullet and still refused to speak English, but we did have a brief and friendly conversation.

I believe I either told her I was fine or that I was a car.

She appeared pleased and either told me it was great to see me again or that I was still —how do you say it in English?—a pathetic monolingual loser with no rhetorical rhythm.

Either way, je m'appelle Abby.

Ou sont les toilettes?

THE GRADUATE

Graduation was overhyped—we all knew it.

It was simply a ceremony you had to go through at the end of four years of awkward moments and hours of academic effort. The last few weeks *(and by weeks, I mean months)* were simply gravy, going through the motions of showing up to ceramics and an English honor's class taught by a teacher resembling a haggard Meryl Streep who included sexual innuendo into every lecture and project assigned.

Since I was proficient in skipping, we'll keep the streak alive and skip past those years for now.

I was actually out of school the final two weeks of my senior year due to an unfortunate incident involving my wisdom teeth, emergency surgery and a head that morphed to much more Ernie than Bert. It was not fun or attractive—much like the aforementioned randy English teacher.

That unfortunate incident was closely followed by a bout with pharyngitis. I know—it was a delightful month or so to be me. I tell you these details not for sympathy—*although donations are always accepted*—but because they all led up to me feeling rather under the weather come graduation day.

But I was a trooper—*or forced to go, the details are fuzzy*—and after a pre-graduation dinner with my family and best friend, we set off for the ceremony.

Now picture hundreds of graduates shoved into a stuffy hallway outside of the auditorium for what seemed like days, the smell of body spray and lotion vainly trying to mask the smell of smoke.

I started to feel funny—lightheaded and very, very warm.

The noise around me dulled to a muted din, but I could read the lips of my best friend as she asked me if I was alright *(or maybe she asked me if I had a light or that I was quite a sight—again, the details are fuzzy.)*

The next thing I knew, I was lying in a pool of sweat on the ground with a headache and no idea why. All I knew was that there was a crowd of *(still blurry)* faces looking on. People rushed to my side and started asking me questions and fanning me with caps and papers.

I was sure they all looked up my dress.

After being reassured that the perverts were at bay, I was taken to the training room and seen by the on-call paramedic while my classmates received their diplomas.

I, on the other hand, received my diploma from the paramedic.

The next day I was fine in that I didn't have any teeth extracted from my head, the equivalent of strep throat with a migraine or the experience of passing out before a graduation ceremony.

In fact, I felt much better. While resting on the couch in my cap and gown—*I had to wear it sometime right?*—I decided that 12 years from then I would blog about that experience in an effort to break out of blogger's block. OK, maybe I made that last part up, but I really did get my diploma from the paramedic.

And I'm pretty sure he never looked up my dress.

SUMMER RHYME TIME

An ode to summer.

Long gone are the mornings spent scraping off snow,

wearing our hats and gloves each place we go.

Flip-flops *(or no shoes)* replace our big boots,

and out come the T-shirts and bright bathing suits.

But when I was a kid summer meant a bit more,

you never quite knew what fun could be in store.

No school to attend and no homework to do,

or boring assemblies left to sit through.

Instead I would sit on my bike or the swings,

falling in rosebushes, icing bruised things.

Wiffle ball games were held back in the grass,

so that it would hurt less to slide on your ass.

The arguments came with about every play,

as someone who sucked at the game would then say:

"I so wasn't out, you can all go to hell,

get off of my property before I tell."

Running through sprinklers and stepping on bees,

Skateboarding fearlessly, skinning our knees.

The trampoline served as a real launching point,

as we "popcorned" each other right out of the joint.

Over the fence they would fly with great height,

setting new records for seconds in flight.

Slip and splash basically served as a way

to quickly maim someone through innocent play.

A water-slicked tarp leading straight down a hill?

A highway to taking one hell of a spill.

Trucks all pimped out with some music and lights,

would sell us kids all kinds of frozen delights.

(Looking back now I think most of those rides

were really a front to sell pot on the side.)

At any rate, we ate our treats in a cone,

our parents bought brownies and left us alone.

We always would find that one friend with a pool,

(the one that we never hung out with at school.)

Camping's been talked about here once before,

but it's simply a summer thing I can't ignore.

For I still remember the fear and the fright,

when told of the Hook Man each hot summer night.

Thanks to the moron who told me that bit,

I was waiting for serial killers to hit.

Now that I'm older and work every day,

this "job" that I speak of just gets in the way.

Work on my tan is replaced with real stuff,

like deadlines and editing drafts that are rough.

But things balance things out with the sunshine and heat,

flowers in bloom and the market with treats.

My skin glows with color and freckles appear,

that normally hide for the rest of the year.

The smell of a charcoal grill still can't be beat,

even though I'm not into consumption of meat.

Things can get steamy, uncomfortably so,

but at least I'm not shoveling three feet of snow.

So while things are different for whatever reason,

summer is still quite a wonderful season.

I might not get weeks off but with any luck,

I soon will cross paths with that great ice cream truck.

(For ice cream, of course.)

EXERCISE TV AND ME

From running "Get in Shape Girl" sessions on my front lawn when I was little to working in a gym for years, exercise has always played a large role I my life.

In the early years, my basement made the transformation from Barbie wonderland/psych ward to aerobics studio, where at any one time I was doing step aerobics videos with the enthusiasm of a manic ex-cheerleader "turn stepping" for her glory days or getting my Body In Motion with Gilad on the beaches of Hawaii.

These daily exercise shows became something I looked forward to, not because I was on a mission to lose weight—far from it—but because I was/am an attention whore and the coordinated routines and music made me feel like I was part of some great off, off, off Broadway performance.

I would sing and Sweat to the Oldies with Richard Simmons or exert my leadership skills by doing the Denise Austin step aerobics tape with the sound off, conducting the class by memory down to the little fake laughs and cheesy sentiments Denise would add in for encouragement.

Those early days were all about the fun and fitness factor—I loved dancing around and working at something while knowing it was good for me. Plus, I loved being bossy, so it worked out well—pun intended.

Now that I'm older I've noticed a couple things about these exercise shows that I hadn't noticed before:

1. The instructors are a special kind of crazy

Aside from the boundless energy and Day-Glo white teeth, they basically spend the whole show carrying on complete conversations about you—asking questions, reminding you that no one likes saggy arms and shouting out encouragement—all without waiting for or acknowledging your reply.

Plus, they never let the pips in the background get a word in edgewise.

2. The fitness world is a melting pot, and they set out to prove it

Back in the days of Gilad, it was usually him on the beach with some busty women in thong leotards with a few old people *(not in thong leotards)* thrown in for good measure. These days, programs are much more politically correct.

If you don't have three distinctly different looking people—perhaps a blond, an African American and a brunette and/or male—doing jumping jacks and push-ups, it obviously means that you hate America and think only white people should be instructed to squeeze and crack a walnut with their ass cheeks.

3. The videos make you feel great no matter what

Because of those one-sided conversations and the instructor's never-ending faith in your dedication to their instruction, you end up feeling great after the show is done, regardless of whether or not you actually lunge or pretend to jump rope.

You can literally turn the TV show on, sit on the couch with a pizza and still have the instructors tell you you're looking great, that you're going to be fit and toned in no time and that you are far superior to those who didn't just spend 30 minutes jumping around like a Polish pinball.

In other words, if your ass doesn't get a boost, at least your ego will.

So even though I'm older now and my fitness interests have evolved a bit, I like knowing that some things never change—namely fitness shows. I can still dance around my living room and act like a manic cheerleader cracked out on spirit all in the name of fitness, much like I did as a ~~precarious~~ spastic youth so many years ago.

The only real difference is that I have a harder time convincing people to participate in my "Get in Shape Girl" sessions on the front lawn these days.

Perhaps I should drop the thong leotard complete with fashionable black belt, but then again, I refuse to compromise my integrity.

DOG DAY DETOUR

With a phone interview for a job in 10 minutes, I was almost home when a dog on the street brought my thoughts back to Earth. Skin and bones, a soiled white, the ragged Pit Bull stood as a stark contrast to the neighborhood.

I slowed down my truck. She slowed down as well.

I looked at the clock. She looked so confused.

First lesson: Think with your heart and not just your head.

This dog was obviously dropped off on our street, callously left to fend for herself in an unfamiliar territory.

She didn't know this. I did.

Pulling in the closest driveway, I got out and realized I had nothing I needed. No collar, no blanket, no leash.

Second lesson: Where there's a will, there's a way.

I did have dog treats and something that resembled a leash of sorts in the backseat of my Blazer, but with no collar I was forced to get creative. She must have sensed my good will, or the opportunity for free food, as she was sweet as could be and cautiously approached me.

Her nails were jagged and long; her delicate face was soiled and scratched, eyes filled with a look of confusion and hopeful trust; her ribs jutted out like prison bars.

I gave her a treat.

There was no struggle when I threw my makeshift collar/leash around her neck and led her to the truck. I dropped the hatch and spent the next five minutes trying to convince this dog that jumping into the back end was the plan.

She didn't know this. I did.

After hefting her front paws on the tailgate, I was able to boost her massive frame into the back. I gave her a treat.

Off we went.

Third lesson: Homeless dogs will not be content being shoved in the back of a Blazer—and they stink. A lot.

Three seconds into the journey, my canine companion decided to fling herself from the back of the Blazer to the passenger's seat.

She wasn't into sticking her head out the open window on her side, but she was into sticking her head out the window on my side. Nails digging into my legs, dirty hair shedding across my lap, the makeshift collar doing nothing to restrain her.

We eventually made it to the Humane Society, where after some paperwork she was turned over to the competent staff that would eventually clean her up, trim those nails and prepare her for her new life.

Fourth lesson: There are still people who understand that life happens—usually to me at the most inopportune time.

I drove back home and prepared myself for the call in which I had to explain to a prospective employer that I missed our phone interview because I was detoured rescuing a homeless Pit Bull from the not-so-mean streets of northwest Grand Rapids.

I didn't think giving her a treat would work.

She understood. We rescheduled, most likely under her assumption that even if I was making up the story, those creative powers could be editorially harnessed and come in handy on the job. I'm not sure.

Either way, I got the job.

The dog got a home.

Detour taken.

Lessons learned.

MY FUZZY LITTLE SOUL SISTER

This is Wendell.

Wendell is 16 years old, and even though I moved out of my mom's house a couple of years ago, I still consider her my cat.

She was homeless and rescued as a kitten, taken in by my mom and named after a song about a homeless man—Mr. Wendell—from an obscure band that was popular for an hour when I was in sixth grade.

I'm pretty sure her senility has kept her from noticing my absence, but it could just be her arrogance refusing to acknowledge my move all of three miles away. When I stop by she will occasionally make an effort to say hello, if it's convenient for her, and it recently occurred to me that even though she only has one tooth, matted hair and a crooked crotch—we're actually a lot alike.

Behold the evidence:

The Hermit Stage

We enjoyed her company for a good 8-9 years before she decided to disappear for a spell, surfacing only to occasionally eat, use the litter box and let us know precisely how uninterested she was in our existence.

As she aged, she went through a "rebirth" of sorts and emerged as a spry yet slightly senile and skinnier version of her former self. For the past couple years she's been happy, fun and entertaining again, if not a little prone to selective hearing and occasional undereating.

Attitude

When it comes to dealing with others, she takes no shit. Don't bother ~~me~~ her when ~~I'm~~ she's sleeping, don't bother her when she's eating and don't bother her if she's going to the bathroom. If you follow those rules, you're probably safe.

She'll let you know if you're not.

Social Skills

She's perceived as antisocial at times, but is really quite the opposite and has a great heart.

When people try to get close to her, she often runs away until it's convenient for her. But if ignored, she will make her presence known through subtle physical cues—a vocal range of noises that make sense only to her and/or awkward physical gestures that may include swipes with unmanicured claws or vain attempts to bite that result in a pathetic painless gumming.

* For the record, we will apply the gumming and clawing to me in a metaphorical sense, as even though I don't get manicures and have all of my teeth, I have yet to resort to blatant physical attacks.

Yet.

Picky Palette

Even though she's thin, she will only eat organic dry cat food and occasional treats as her mood will allow. While she's been offered a variety of brands and options to try, she's dead-set on organic or nothing at all. Budget be damned.

Thrill of the Hunt

She loves it.

When the mood hits and a bug appears, she will delight in chasing a fly around. Batting it here and trapping it there, she will let it escape before claiming her dominance once again. Once she gets it—the fly and the reassurance that she still has it—she gets bored and moves on.

Extracurricular Activities

Catnip makes her happy and she's very content to lick herself *(and appears to neither desire nor require a partner in this activity.)*

*No comment.

Easily Amused

She finds joy in eating, sleeping, lying in a patch of sun and aimlessly chasing after the light from a laser pen or a reflection on the wall. And as we know, I do as well.

Of course we have our differences—namely the fact that she's a cat with only one tooth, matted hair and a crooked crotch—but some are more subtle.

- I have two legs and she has four, four that are quite hairy. While I've never "enjoyed" shaving—*and would question anyone who does, quite frankly*—I take this female burden in stride. She opts to play the feline vs. female card and has never voluntarily had her excessive body hair removed.

- Financially speaking, she's basically played the "I was homeless and orphaned" card for 16 years, meaning she's never had a job, paid taxes or contributed monetarily to the household.

While we differ in that respect, I have to give her props for pulling it off so well.

- Finally, she doesn't enjoy the outdoors. Attempts to put her on a leash and roam the backyard have resulted in not-so subtle physical cues—a vocal range of ungodly loud noises and ninja-like physical gestures that included swipes with unmanicured claws, bites that resulted in somehow breaking skin with the one tooth that she has and an unpleasant spraying of urine *(hers, not mine.)*

Although we have our differences, I love the little one-toothed wonder. So when I stop by I occasionally make an effort to say hello—if it's convenient for her, of course—brush her a bit and offer some catnip.

With us Leos, flattery won't get you everywhere, but it can get your furry foot in the door.

After all, it takes one to know one.

YES, I'M NOSY

Along with being kind of large, my nose is prone to bleeding in the winter months when the air is dry. No, I don't pick my nose and cause it to bleed as so many people remark. But rather the simple act of inhaling and exhaling—*rather necessary, I might add* — or the occasional nose blowing can cause a nosebleed.

It's not a big deal at all, other than being an inconvenience, which it totally was last night when I got one while shoveling my driveway with the ferocity of a manic gnat with roid rage. My quest to remove the frozen slush was interrupted by what I thought was the typical "noseous runneous" so common when outside at night in the winter.

Red snow is a bit scarier than yellow snow. Don't eat either of them.

So I found myself inside, lying on my back in the bathroom staring at my ceiling, tending to what I prefer to call an overuse injury. While I was studying the shower curtain liner, it occurred to me that I've never talked about my nose on here. Considering it was basically begging for attention at that moment in time, I figured I might as well.

The thing is, I've never really had traditional body image issues. I know that sounds weird coming from someone "with issues," but if you've known me for more than five minutes, you know the deal. But I have always had a part of my body that I was very self-conscious of—not my legs, not my stomach, but my nose.

See, it's kind of big and had a bump in the middle of it.

Ever since it matured, I've despised it and wondered why I couldn't get matching bumps a bit lower instead. I would cover my nose up in pictures to see what I would look like with a "normal" nose, started

122

researching rhinoplasty when I was nine and too smart for my own good and went out of my way to make sure my profile was minimally photographed.

My mom always told me I was nuts, but there were a few kids that validated this insecurity for me *(the nose, not the mental instability.)* Middle school was the worst. I admit I didn't help myself with bad perms and questionable fashion choices, but that awkward phase is made even more awkward when your insecurity is literally staring you in the face— and if you're a loud sneezer.

High school was better and I kind of grew used to it. I actually got a body to distract from the schnoz and developed a personality that slowly found validation in things I did and not in how I looked from the side.

It was — and still is — one of my biggest body image issues.

But as my nose matured, so did I. The nose I have is the same nose that my grandpa had, my mom has and a majority of my aunts, uncles and cousins have. Along with kielbasa, chrusciki, a love of baseball and politically incorrect humor, carrying on this Polish protuberance is sort of like a family seal.

Do I love it? Heck no, but with a few exceptions, I do love my family. When I started to look at the profile of my nose instead of my nose in profile, my obsession over it slowly went away. Plus, it's kind of important for that whole breathing thing. Barring a few nosebleeds, it does its job well.

But if offered would I get a nose job today?

Nope, and not just because I'm cheap. But grandma didn't pass along her ample boobs, so those puppies are up for grabs.

Figuratively, of course.

A GOOD NINE LIVES

Wendell, my Fuzzy Little Soul Sister, reached the end of all nine of her lives this week.

However, this isn't a sad post—I promise. When it comes to death, I think a little bit differently than most people. I can usually frame it in a "circle of life" type of way. It's inevitable, and instead of fighting it or fearing it, I tend to accept it.

But I'm still sad.

Anyway, Wendell the One-Toothed Wonder Cat's situation just called to mind memories of pets gone by and some interesting circumstances surrounding their departure.

Keep in mind the fact that my mom is Dr. Doolittle and it's normal for us to spend two hours coaxing a chipmunk out of a drainage pipe in 90 degree heat *(he made it out safe, if not a bit dazed and confused)*, chasing a loose goat through briar patches *(I made it out safe, if not a bit dazed and confused)* or picking up stray dogs on the way to job interviews *(I got nothing for this one—so much for symmetry)*.

We've had tons of animals throughout the years, but these are just a few examples.

I will keep the stories short and sweet, unlike that disclaimer.

- First there was Mitten, aka "Bun," my rabbit when I was in preschool. The creativity for his name was inspired by the fact that he was a bunny with a white mittened foot. "Bun" met an untimely death at the hands of a homicidal cage cleaner—aka "dad"— that "accidently" used harmful chemicals to clean. I was at a friend's house and by the time I got home, the body was already stiff. Determined to bury him in our backyard pet cemetery, holes were cut in a shoebox so his legs could stick out. I think we get points for creativity there.

- In kindergarten, I received the best dog in the world and named him Cromwell *(obviously more sophisticated than Mitten.)* He was a Peke-a-poo and the cutest, most loving thing ever. There was an incident and he had a little crooked nose, but he was awesome. He lived to be about 3,000 in dog years, and when he passed away we had him cremated. He came back in something the size of a business card. I've seen more ashes on a sidewalk outside Starbucks.

- Gonzo, a beautiful cockatiel, joined the family a couple of years later and lived to be about 3,000 in bird years. The little feathered bastard chose to pass away while I was on my first business trip ever *(New York)* a few years ago. My mom had to keep him in the freezer until I could come home and we could have a proper burial. It was very traumatic for all three of us— especially Gonzo.

- Speaking of the freezer, I also had to freeze a dead fish for some people I was house-sitting for. That was awkward.

There are many more stories I could share—a cat getting its head caught in the rails of our dining room chair and me having to butter it to get it out *(not unlike my mom buttering my own head when I was little and got my head caught in the rails of the stairway)* or an accidental archeological find while planting flowers in the pet garden, for example—but I'll leave you with just one more.

- I would often dog sit for some people down the street. They have a big dog and a little mutt that is about 3,000 years old in dog years—Burrie. When I was first introduced to the dogs, I was told that Burrie squatted when he peed instead of lifting his leg. That's not that weird in and of itself, but the reason he squats is because he doesn't have a penis. Apparently he was hit by a car when he was little and it was ripped off, never to be

125

seen again. He was taken to the shelter and was going to be put down, but this family paid for his surgery and adopted him. I was told by the husband that if his penis ever gets ripped off, he just wants to be put down.

At any rate, Wendell will be missed.

She was buried in the garden cemetery among the many animal companions we've loved and lost throughout the years. We're all sad, but I can't wait for the flowers in that garden to bloom—especially the catnip.

HELP ME PLAN MY MIDLIFE CRISIS

My 30th birthday is next month and before you ask, no, I do not have any wild and crazy plans to commemorate this momentous occasion. I love celebrating birthdays—or random Wednesdays—but I'm not into celebrating my own.

So now that I've put the kabosh on the surprise party you had planned for me, let's move on to the bigger issue—the midlife crisis I am planning.

I'm not sure who decided that 50 was the age when it a midlife crisis was expected to happen. That's being awfully presumptuous, as not that many people live to be 100 and have Williard Scott put their picture on the side of a Smucker's jelly jar, butcher their name and wish them a Happy Birthday.

Considering my propensity for falling up stairs and landing on the one needle in a haystack, I'll be lucky to make it to 50. So even though I don't want to tempt fate, I've optimistically decided to be proactive and use 30 as my mid-life marker.

If I make it to 60, then I can look back at how I was able to accurately cash in on the whole thing. If I make it *past* 60, then I'm really considered and overachiever and everything else is just icing on the (birthday) cake.

It makes perfect sense to me, but then again, so does only buying clothes that will never need ironing.

Anyway, I've been doing a little observational research, and I've found that in order to have this mid-life crisis I'm supposed to do one or all of the things listed below. I haven't quite worked out the details yet, but your suggestions would be most appreciated as soon as possible.

After all, I'm not getting any younger.

Midlife Crisis To-Do List

While purple is my favorite color, I need to adopt a love of yellow and buy expensive yellow things. My research has shown that yellow sports cars and yellow motorcycles are the most common thing to purchase with money the mid-lifer doesn't have.

I'm not into cars, but that's okay because I've also noticed that yellow hair is an acceptable substitute. Male or female, yellow or platinum blond hair that previously wasn't is a sure sign of youth and sends nothing but "I'm not having a midlife crisis and dying my hair out of desperation" vibes.

I've been platinum before, so this is an option to consider once again.

Change of Scenery

Through my research I've found that if I really want to do this crisis right, I have to quit my job and book a flight to Tanzania to climb Kilimanjaro. Despite semi-stable employment *(and the possibility of additional car payments and salon visits,)* I should throw caution to the wind and become one with an extreme challenge in a foreign country.

If I'm lucky and make it to the top, platinum blond hair blowing in the wind, this will evidently prove that I am still a free spirit and physically capable of pushing myself past the boundaries of normal people my age. This would probably be more impressive if I was actually of AARP status and not only 30, so it's possible I should hold off on this until that point.

Hook It Up

I need to have an affair with someone either much older or much younger than me, and I'm torn about which way to go with this one.

If I go the cougar route and rob the cradle, I most certainly benefit from the physical aspects of this relationship. Plus, parading him out in public would be a nice boost to my ego.

However, if I rob the wealthy retirement home, I benefit from the Sugar Daddy aspect and physical demands would be limited to feeding him mechanically processed oat bran with a silver spoon and wiping his chin.

Both are probably looking for someone to take care of them, meaning I'll most likely opt for my continued unrequited love affair with several professional athletes and Daniel Tosh.

Or get a plant.

Crisis Conclusion

I suppose another option is just to embrace my entrance into mid-life and complain about the weather, pretend not to hear people, go to bed early, choose veggies over beer, glare at loud children, gripe about how I miss "real" books and conversation, clip coupons every Sunday and then blog about all these mundane daily events in an attempt to keep my questionable sanity.

Oh crap.

It seems I'm ahead of my time...

MORE...INFINITY

Sometimes I think I'm selfish.

Not in the, "I think only of me" sense at all, but still selfish nonetheless.

I have basically constructed my own little world, in that for the most part I do what I want and am really not accountable to anyone else. Yes, there are family and friends, but there are no children I am responsible for, no husband to check-in with if I'm running late. Yes, I have a boss and responsibilities, but I'm basically working to support myself and my necessities.

This means that at times I don't have to pretend to be anything other than what I'm feeling. If I'm cranky, I don't have to pretend smile and be civil when I come home from work. If I'm tired, I can sleep. If I want to do a yoga tape, I don't have to wait for the TV. In essence, I kind of revolve my world around myself. Even though I give what I can to those I care for, the only one I really have to worry about making happy is me.

I don't hide my emotions well, and to be honest, I think I would find it exhausting to try and live my life that way. But there are times I am humbled, when I push any mood or "disordered" thinking out of my head and simply smile, laugh and talk. While I may not be that way all the time, I can play that role when necessary.

It's been very necessary lately with my grandma.

While details aren't needed, let's just say the relationship between her, my mom and me is about as tight as three generations can go. That's a good thing and a bad thing, as my mom deals with grandma craziness and I deal with a double dose from both of them. However, I can play that role when necessary.

Gram is 86 and I've pretty much prepared myself for her death the past few years, actually since my grandpa passed away eight years ago. They had done everything they ever wanted to do—created a business, a huge family, a life together for more than 60 years—and were so completely at peace *(you wouldn't know it by how they argued, but it was all part of the deal.)*

So as bad as it sounds, when she goes I'll be fine. Even though I have an odd perspective on death in general *(as in, it doesn't really bother me)*, things have been getting so bad that it will actually be a relief when it happens. But with each passing day it gets closer and closer and each day it can take its toll.

It finally hit my mom last night. *(Background—she's an extremely emotional person. I am the complete opposite, ironically.)* I was making a dessert at my mom's when she came back from the home; she goes every day. Something last night hit her hard and she lost it. I can't say much, as she doesn't really understand my "I'm at peace with things" attitude at times like these, but sometimes you don't have to say anything at all. By the time I cleaned up she was fine. We have this silent understanding when it comes to emotions.

I had plans of an evening walk or yoga tape — of course I need my exercise — but instead I ran over to the home and watched some of the game with Gram *(we get our love of baseball from her.)* I smiled. I talked a little about my day. She listened and continued to fiddle with her hands a bit as she's taken to doing lately.

I brushed her hair, now so brittle and thin, for half an hour. I massaged her arms and swollen legs as best as I could with her sitting in her chair. I knew she didn't care how her hair looked, if I was clumsy in my efforts at massage, if I got my walk in that day.

All she knew was she loved how it felt.

Her eyes were closed and for once, I didn't try and fill the silence. With the game in the background, I didn't make my normal conversation. I just let her be quiet. I just let me be quiet. I watched her enjoy this simple pleasure, as minor as it was, and for that hour I put away any "to-do's" I had planned for the night. I didn't care how I hair looked, if I was clumsy in my efforts at massage, if I got my walk in that day.

All she knew was she loved how it felt.

They came to get her for her bath, but before I left I took her face in my hands and kissed her, telling her I love her like I always do. As she always does, she replied back that she loves me more. We go back and forth with our argument until one of us gives in *(or I leave and shut the door yelling "More!")*

This time her voice was a little weaker, and mine might have been, too. Yes, I have basically constructed my own little world, but she's been a huge part of it for all of my life.

And she always will be, more…infinity.

-written July 2010

SENIOR MOMENTS

Contrary to popular belief, I actually have quite a few friends.

True, most of them don't remember my name five minutes after I talk *(loudly and repeatedly)* to them. They often can't fend for themselves in basic ways — food, drinks, the bathroom — and concern about personal appearance *(and unfortunately in some cases, personal hygiene)* is virtually non-existent.

While I realize this could probably describe a majority of people I went to college with, I am actually referring to the senior citizens under 24-hour medical care at my grandma's senior community/residential/hospital facility. That sounds formal, so we'll just go with old people.

They don't mind when I say that, and if they do, they'll forget five minutes later anyway.

I've talked about the relationship between my mom, my grandma and me before, so we won't bring that back up. But if you're just joining us, we're pretty close—three generations of Polish snark not lacking authenticity or attitude—for better or for worse. My mom goes to see her every day and I generally go around her suppertime a few times a week.

The dining room is where our adventures will take us today.

Fill a dining room with 25 old people, dementia, 20 wheelchairs, chair alarms, oxygen tanks, "clothing protectors *(bibs),* dietary restrictions and no verbal filter within a 50-foot radius and you have yourself a reality show that will never be made, although perhaps it should.

So until I figure out how to add a few midgets, a cake competition or a rehabbing D-list celebrity to the mix to entice TLC to pick it up, I thought I would share a few observations and snippets of conversation from the last week alone.

There's no way I could ever touch on the genius that is my grandma, so she is mostly excluded from these examples. However, she makes an appearance. In fact, she always makes an appearance.

In reference to his hot dog dinner, 85-year old Leon will proclaim that his "wiener is limp." His wife will reply with, "It has been for years, but I stuck around anyway." True love.

Every time Leon asks to be wheeled back to his room before anyone else, Gram interjects (from her wheelchair) with "There goes the president. Big Shit McGee."

At the same table, Richard took a moment to educate us on the fact that the president has decided to let everyone smoke marijuana legally now. This is not really groundbreaking news for Richard though, as apparently he has been smoking marijuana since the war and shared that it tends to make him paranoid.

At which point Gram looked at me and said, "He's not paranoid. We do all want him to shut his goddamn mouth."

There was a minor incident when Richard "allegedly" left the table without properly saying goodbye to Chet. Chet announced he would not be talking to Richard tomorrow and proceeded to steal a tater tot from Richard's plate.

A tater tot was later thrown across the room in a rather impressive arc given the waning athletic abilities of the elderly. I am not accusing anyone...Chet.

Carrots were the topic of ridicule and disgust one evening, as they were proclaimed to be "disgusting rabbit food," "orange crap" and "shit I wouldn't feed a dead dog" by three separate women.

Keep in mind that at least one of these women is still of the mind that if meat is cooked, it no longer has to be refrigerated. Ever. In fact, it can be left out directly in the sun...Gram.

Mashed up pills are mixed in with pudding. Mashed up pills mixed in with pudding are spit out, most likely by the same resident(s) that will wait with bated breath for the metal dessert cart to be wheeled into the dining room. If there is no pudding, chaos may ensue.

Back at Gram's table, Margarite will eat four bites of her dinner before dozing off and knocking her oxygen tube out of her nose, waking her up just in time for dessert. She never misses dessert. She also doesn't say much, but this could be because Gram—with a mouthful of food herself— is usually harping on her to eat more than four bites of her dinner.

This is purely a formality, as Gram will wait until Margarite dozes off to tell me to take the extra packages of unopened crackers and French Vanilla coffee creamer from her spot. Like a chipmunk, Gram will store these supplies in case of a club cracker famine in the coming months.

Like clockwork, Julia at the table behind us will get up five minutes into the meal and set off her chair alarm. Every night she's told to wait, but every night she stands up and complains about the noisy beeps that follow.

At this point, I have to give Gram a "look" and make sure she doesn't offer helpful advice to Julia about "sitting her ass down for cripe's sake" or shaking the ants out of her pants. I am usually unsuccessful.

This same *(ever-so shy)* woman will loudly proclaim that new male nurse passing out drugs in the pudding is actually a woman. How does she know this? Because there was a bowling tournament and when he had to use the bathroom, they had to change the sign on the door to accommodate his "condition." Plus, "he talks like a queer."

He/she will not overhear this, although the other aides will and will find this highly amusing. Apparently "Bruce" and his aloof attitude are not well-liked in the senior community, whereas this very shy and quiet woman is basically a rock star in the eyes of the staff.

An unintentional game of geriatric Marco Polo will be played across the room, while behind us the gossipy table of women will complain about the food being too hot or too cold, the horrible hair style Agnus is sporting *(the one in the deluxe wheelchair being fed through a straw)* and how they just don't understand why so-and-so couldn't meet them for that game of cards today.

"Dialysis is no excuse. She's just being rude."

A priest will clutch his nightly bottle of root beer like a Budweiser and refuse to let go until the last drop is gone, even if it requires a straw, which it usually does. Requests will be made on the sly for me to add a secret shot of vodka to their cranberry juice refills.

*If they tipped, I might consider it.

Once the last crumb of "crap cakes" has been consumed and the "clothing protector" has been removed, I then have to attempt to maneuver Gram's horrifically awkward wheelchair out of the dining hall and down to her room before her "dupa" explodes. This activity is about as complicated as a secret ops mission involving a tank and hidden landmines.

And I always make sure to say good-bye to Chet, as we wouldn't want to incite another tater tot torpedo.

Gram can—and most likely will—do that on her own.

So, this was simply the past week or so and fails to include the time the fire alarm went off and diners complained about the loud "music," any references to bodily functions *(and oh yes, they are rampant)* or other conspiracy theories that reside in a pile of peas.

There are many, many senior moments.

And please keep in mind that I love these people, as *(most of them)* have good hearts *(emotionally, not necessarily physically)* and good intentions. They make me laugh, they get me out of my head and if nothing else, they make me feel better about going to bed by 10 pm and actually liking prunes.

Prunes are highly underrated.

So are old people.

I will never forget my senior moments.

SENIOR MOMENTS: BINGO

Have you ever spent the night playing Bingo with 25 people over the age of 75 on the medical side of an assisted living facility? If not, I'll let you in on just what you're missing.

In the next installment of "Senior Moments," we will go to the activity room.

I'll set the scene:

It's four people to a table, two cards to a person, one bowl of Bingo chips for each player. Wheelchairs are locked and they're ready to roll.

This seems innocent enough, but let's get one thing straight.

These people have been through wars, marriages, children, deaths, Depressions and depressions. Now they no longer worry about recessions as much as they do if Gertrude next door stole the extra Nutter Butter from their snack tray last Thursday.

My point? They've got nothing to lose and they play for keeps. Or rather, they play for candy, which along with popcorn, is the geriatric equivalent of crack.

The activity director—a small, demure blonde girl with a huge heart—will call out the numbers like an NFL quarterback calling a play.

"B 14," the caller will say. "B one four."

Someone will ask "before what?" while at least two others will mistake "B14" for something either in the "N" column or as a directive to complain about the fact that it was supposed to be beer and popcorn night.

More numbers will be called and silence—save for a few rogue coughs or bodily functions—will blanket the room. This is either due to the fact that concentration is required for placing each chip, or that half of them have forgotten what they're doing.

"O 63," the caller will say. "O six three."

Mary, sitting right next to the caller, will ask her what was said. This will be repeated after every number called, annoying Gram who will passive-aggressively express this annoyance with a Morse Code of exasperated sighs and Polish cursing.

I will have to remind her that Mary is 100 years old, to which Gram will reply that after 100 years, she should know her way around a goddamn Bingo card.

Leona will win twice in a row, pretty much guaranteeing evil glares and a public shunning by the women until she repents in some way— throwing a game or throwing a hip—to get herself back in good graces.

This might sound harsh, but remember, candy is at stake.

After each triumphant "Bingo!" is called, my mom will distribute that candy by prancing around the room with a tray like an old-fashioned cigarette girl in a bar.

(With the exception of June, who will be given a pudding cup if she's fortunate enough to win, as she is unfortunately on a puree diet.)

The winner will go one of two ways—either directly for the junk food jugular by grabbing their favorite chocolate-covered treats, or the less manic route, pondering this decision as if a Twix is the last thing they will ever eat in their life.

Which, to be fair, just might be true.

After everyone's told that their cards must be cleared, the next round of play will begin.

"G 55," the caller will say. "G five five."

Mary will ask what was said, Gram will sigh heavily enough to move Julia's card across the table and Leona will hide the fact that both of her cards contain G55. Out of nowhere Richard will ask where the beer and popcorn are and where the waitress went.

I will remark that a beer sounds good, at which point Gram will remind me that if I wasn't so picky, I could be out drinking beer with a nice man like Richard or the maintenance man who hung the shelf in her room last week.

I will have to remind her that Richard is 94 years old and the maintenance man was actually a very butch woman, to which Gram will reply that after 30 years, I should lower my standards.

"O66," the caller will say. "O six six."

But then I would miss all the fun.

OUR SCARS

This piece was written about my mom in response to a prompt about finding beauty in something perceived as ugly (like a scar.)

In rare times of frustration and brief self-despair,

She claims she is broken and beyond repair.

From surgeries more numerous than fingers to count,

She has her scars on the inside and out.

A neck and a spinal cord basically fused,

Excuses to dwell on this always refused.

Body casts, braces were part of her life,

Part of her role as a mother and wife.

For me I thought surgery was part of the norm,

Something all moms did in one shape or form.

Hiding her scars on the inside and out,

With clothes that concealed and no signs of self-doubt.

In fact, she was always the fun one to see,

The mom on the block you wish your mom could be.

Baseball in summer and raking in fall,

Snowmen in winter and trips to the mall.

Even if she couldn't do it herself,

(Limited as she was in her own health,)

She made sure all the kids had more fun than they should,

Doing the things that she wished that she could.

I never quite realized the struggles she had,

Physically, mentally, feeling so bad.

As time has gone by I see more of her pain,

Taking it on as my own, yet in vain.

She thinks they are ugly, these scars that she wears,

Constant reminders of what she must bear.

A physical flaw isn't what comes to mind,

When I see her scars or a mark of that kind.

The scars tell a story of one woman's life,

As a mother, a daughter, a sister, a wife.

It's flawed and not perfect, with times of self-doubt,

But beautiful still, on the inside and out.

SENIOR MOMENTS: OPENING DAY

Today we will be moving from dining room drama to Opening Day of baseball season in the activity room.

If you know anything about me or my family—I tend to overshare here—you know that there are no bigger sports fans than me, my mom and my grandma (G.) Needless to say, I am super excited that baseball season has started, and considering I don't get excited about much other than food, sunshine and sleeping—preferably in the sunshine—this shows the magnitude of my love of the game.

And much like the bump on my nose, the love of the game is genetic.

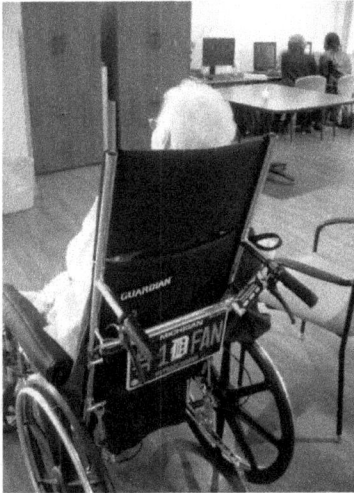

Even though she can't remember what day it is, G can tell you who played first base in 1968 and who pitched the third game of the World Series. This is the woman who Ernie Harwell knew by name at the

143

games and who kept a mini souvenir Tiger bat under the seat of her Cadillac to ward off hoodlums that drove white vans with no windows.

So per tradition, I took the afternoon off of work to watch the game with mom and G. At first it was just the three of us. Then another resident got wheeled in, then another, then another until there were close to 10 residents and a few nurses—all women—watching the game.

It wasn't like being at the ballpark or at a sports bar, but that's not necessarily a bad thing—especially for me, considering my desire for social interaction is limited to the clerk at the grocery store.

A quick recap:

- The crowd was comparably demure, most likely due to overmedication and not overconsumption of $8 beer. There was the occasional "whoop!" from me and mom *(normal, but in a much more reserved fashion,)* a "Come on my little sweetheart" or "Goddamn bum" from G *(depending on the situation)* and random bodily noises from various other residents *(normal, but in a much less reserved fashion.)*

- My attempts at the wave were not well-received, or even noticed, as far as I could tell.

- Stadium blankets were not needed, but quilted afghans were placed on the laps of all residents in attendance—despite the fact that it felt like an 85 degree day in that room.

- There were no $5 hot dogs or nachos to buy, but the nurse did come around at snack time with her cart of assorted juices and munchies—free! Mom supplied the Cracker Jacks, a single box of which contained exactly three peanuts and one tattoo among the popcorn.

- Although a resident did have her "baby" *(doll)* with her as usual, there were no screaming children and no tantrums due to cotton candy sugar highs or the denial of overpriced souvenirs. My kind of kid.

- Due to their decreasingly slow reaction times, my efforts to circulate a beach ball through the "stands" was less than successful—even more so than the wave.

- However, the seventh inning stretch included a rousing round of "Take Me Out to the Ballgame" that Harry Caray would have been proud of.

- We had no streakers, but Geraldine did fly by the TV in her wheelchair numerous times throughout the game. She tends to cover a lot of ground when she's on a mission, which is apparently all of the time.

- Finally, when the game was over, there were no crowds of people to wade through or traffic jams to battle. In fact, considering that most of the residents weren't aware that the game was actually over and were nodding off due to the post-lunch pre-nap nap they are accustomed to, they didn't seem to be in a hurry to go anywhere.

So even though it's possible this was a closing chapter on our Opening Day tradition, I wouldn't have had it any other way.

I take that back.

The Tigers could have won and saved us from the post-game overanalysis of a certain 89-year old woman convinced she would have led the team to victory, but then again, it was just another Senior Moment.

And she was quickly distracted with a chocolate bar.

Let the games begin.

MY PERFECT GAME

This won't mean a lot to most of you out there, but this weekend the Detroit Tigers clinched their first division title since 1987, and their first American League Central title ever.

It's kind of a big deal.

But don't worry. This post isn't going to be filled with statistics and names of men being (over)paid to play a boy's sport or ridiculous metaphors about the game that I've loved all my life. If you don't love baseball, you certainly won't love my explanation of why I do. If you do love baseball, you don't need it.

But for me, it's more than a game.

It's remembering summers by games that were played and the sensory clues I still find—the crack of the bat, the stitch on a ball, the smell of the grass in the field. It's looking forward to spring training in the dead of winter when every other joy seems frozen beneath layers of ice and of snow.

It's being able to identify players by their batting stance or jersey number and feeling an instant connection with a complete stranger when I see them wearing a shirt with the old English "D."

It's a simple game—a bat and a ball—but it can unite a city, a state, a family—with one swing of that bat or one pitch of that ball. It can make grown men cry, and sometimes, even a 30-year-old woman who usually one cries for road kill and good food spilled on the floor.

For me, it's my escape.

Sports in general afford me the opportunity to forget about the mundane concerns of everyday life for a while and to spend an unpredictable amount of time with others who take pleasure in enjoying a similar break. It's a reminder that I can still feel excited about something when a lot of the time I'm just numb.

For me, it's family.

It's a 89-year-old woman who can't always remember who I am, but will tell me about a game in 1948 with a clarity time hasn't stolen quite yet.

Some days the games are all foreign to her and she couldn't care less if one's on. Some days watching the game with her takes me right back to being sprawled on her living room floor as a kid, watching each game on mute while Ernie Harwell came through on the radio *(but not lying underneath the ceiling fan, as I was warned the goddamn thing would inevitably fall on me and crush me to death. Fuzzy memories.)*

Because while I joke about her and there are still good times, the bad days outnumber the good by a lot. But on those good days, baseball bridges a gap as we talk of the games and the team. It is tradition and memories tied up with box scores and hopefulness mixed in with stats.

From this year's Opening Day to where we are now, this season has felt somewhat special. And despite my promise not to wax eloquently with corny language, I guess I can't help it. Sure, it's a "pastime," but it's my favorite way to pass that time.

For me, it's more than a game.

It's my *perfect* game.

SENIOR MOMENTS: DATING

It's time for another installment of Senior Moments and the genius that is my 90-year-old grandma. We're back in the dining room again, but this time the meal is not the center of attention, but rather the lack of a beefcake in my life—a subject that has been brought up on more than two *(or 202)* occasions.

Seeing as my grandma was married when she was 18, the fact that I'm 30 and single still baffles her mind. However, at 90 years old, people who refrigerate their perishable items still baffle her mind.

At any rate, I'll set the scene.

It was me, Gram, a resident we'll call J and her *(single, middle-aged)* daughter, B at the table—the usual crew. The nurse doing meds in the dining room was not a crowd favorite, and Gram loudly proclaimed her to be a pain in the ass multiple times throughout the meal. I didn't tell her to be nice. The nurse is a pain in the ass.

The pain in the ass walked by our table and in a fake smile on her face and told J she was looking nice. Gram looked at her with disgust, picked up her fork and pointed it at J before saying, "That woman can eat shit."

I grabbed Gram's arm and did the, "Gram, shush" thing before she dared me to "shush" her again with her death stare usually reserved for ballgames and people trying to take away her mashed potatoes.

"She can eat shit," Gram continued, keeping her eyes on me before looking back at J, "because J knows she looks nice every day. She doesn't need that pain in the ass to tell her that."

I was glad I didn't shush her.

With that she winked at J, set down her fork and proceeded to go on dispensing advice like a Polish Dr. Laura. Apparently two of the young aids were talking to Gram about dating that week, something she felt the need to tell me and B about over her pistachio pudding pie and coffee.

We were told the following things:

- When I was younger, it was about finding a good Polish man. If you were bored, it was because you were too picky or not trying hard enough. If he's boring, go bowling with him. There's nothing boring about bowling. Just remember to let him win once or twice.

- Don't be so stubborn. He doesn't have to look like a movie star or make a lot of money. You don't want ugly kids, but if you wait too long, you won't have any kids at all.

B and I met eyes at this, and it's possible I rolled mine, prompting Gram to say, "Did I mention *you* by name? Did I say that *you're* too old and too picky?" before moving on with a shrug.

- You have to spice things up. I remember your grandpa would come downstairs while I was doing the washing and bend me over the washing machine. Sometimes I was annoyed, but it never lasted long enough for me to care.

- If you're in a car with a man and he starts to get fresh with his hands, tell him to knock it off. If he doesn't listen, open the door and kick his ass out of the car. Tell him to go find a floosy on the avenue and then take yourself out for ice cream.

With that she returned her focus back to finishing her coffee before leaning over and conspiratorially whispering, "Abby, come here. You see that woman at the table across from us?"

I looked and saw the same 85-year-old woman that always sat across from us gumming at a cookie.

149

"Look at how her bra strap is showing and her shirt is falling down," Gram said with disgust, wiping her hand on her John Deere "clothing protector" before continuing. "Men don't find that attractive. It's sloppy. Take note of that."

"I don't think she even knows it's showing Gram, as her oxygen tube probably moves her shirt around," I said, not adding that an 85-year-old woman was probably not trying to snag a man when she couldn't even snag a pea with a fork.

"That's no excuse," Gram said with a scoff. "She looks cheap."

A male aid walked up and wheeled the senior slut away, providing an opportunity for Gram to tell me that when she was my age, "Well, I would have been married for 12 years at that point, but if I wasn't, I would sink my clamps into that beefcake."

Drained of the will to argue much more or explain that the definition of "beefcake" for a 30-year-old woman in 2011 wasn't a homosexual male nurse with bigger boobs than my own, I simply looked at her and felt a wave of affection wash over me.

"Gram, come here," I whispered conspiratorially. "I love you."

She turned to me and with said with a sigh, "Abbuchucka, I love you so much that it hurts."

She was quiet for a moment before adding, "Then again, that might just be gas from the crap that I ate."

With that I gave her a kiss, smoothed back her hair and told her I had to head home. She gave me the standard warning to be careful and not pick up any strange men.

"Then again," she said with a wink, "maybe you should just take what you can get."

Well played, old woman, well played.

A TOAST

I would like to propose a toast—to the Detroit Tigers toaster my mom and stepdad gave me for my birthday and for everything nice anyone has ever done for me.

That includes you for reading this.

ABOUT THE AUTHOR

Abby Heugel is a writer and aspiring hermit in Michigan who is waiting to be discovered as either a brilliant writer, Broadway star or professional asparagus eater. She can't sing very well, so she's hoping the other two pan out.

You can read more of Abby's work at http://abbyhasissues.com/.

Twitter: @abbyhasissues
Facebook: Abby Has Issues

www.ingramcontent.com/pod-product-compliance
Lightning Source LLC
Chambersburg PA
CBHW071000040426
42443CB00007B/595